Hunger for Understanding

Hunger for Understanding

A workbook for helping young people
to understand and overcome
anorexia nervosa

Alison Eivors and Sophie Nesbitt

JOHN WILEY & SONS, LTD

Other Wiley Editorial Offices

John Wiley & Sons Inc., 111 River Street, Hoboken, NJ 07030, USA

Jossey-Bass, 989 Market Street, San Francisco, CA 94103-1741, USA

Wiley-VCH Verlag GmbH, Boschstr. 12, D-69469 Weinheim, Germany

John Wiley & Sons Australia Ltd, 33 Park Road, Milton, Queensland 4064, Australia

John Wiley & Sons (Asia) Pte Ltd, 2 Clementi Loop #02-01, Jin Xing Distripark, Singapore
129809

John Wiley & Sons Canada Ltd, 22 Worcester Road, Etobicoke, Ontario, Canada M9W 1L1

Wiley also publishes its books in a variety of electronic formats. Some content that appears in
print may not be available in electronic books.

British Library Cataloguing in Publication Data
A catalogue record for this book is available from the British Library

ISBN-13 978-0-470-02128-6 (pbk)
ISBN-10 0-470-02128-4 (pbk)

Typeset in 10/13pt Scala and Scala Sans by SNP Best-set Typesetter Ltd., Hong Kong.
Printed and bound in Great Britain by Antony Rowe Ltd, Chippenham, Wiltshire.
This book is printed on acid-free paper responsibly manufactured from sustainable forestry in
which at least two trees are planted for each one used for paper production.

Contents

About the authors

Alison Eivors qualified as a clinical psychologist in 1999. During her training she developed an interest in eating disorders and completed her doctorate in this area. She conducted a qualitative study that investigated reasons for dropout from services for anorexia nervosa. This gave her the opportunity to interview women about the meaning of their eating difficulties and gave her an invaluable insight into the very functional role anorexia can play in people's lives and the enormous battle they face to overcome the disorder.

Alison currently works as Principal Clinical Psychologist at a specialist adolescent mental health service in Leicester. This post has provided her with the opportunity to work clinically with young women suffering from eating disorders.

For the past two years Alison has been part of a multidisciplinary team to review her local service for young people with eating disorders. The review involved researching the evidence base, interviewing previous clients and visiting other specialist units around the country. This has drawn her attention to the need for creative and varied therapeutic techniques (such as psycho-education, motivational-enhancement and cognitive-behavioural techniques) in the treatment of young people with anorexia.

Sophie Nesbitt developed a special interest in working with young people with eating disorders while working as a trainee clinical psychologist. Her doctorate research investigated the role of exercise as a risk factor in the development and maintenance of eating disorders. She was also able to work clinically with young people with eating disorders at an inpatient unit. Much of this work involved working and communicating effectively with young people, and she developed a particular interest in the development of psycho-education information for this client group.

Sophie is currently working in a multidisciplinary outpatient team. This provides her with the opportunity to work with other types of disorders, such as developmental disorders and emotional disorders. However, as part of this post she is also involved in training other healthcare professionals in generic mental health issues. By necessity, a large part of this training has focused on raising awareness of eating disorders within primary care settings.

Sophie is also currently involved in a preliminary research study aimed at evaluating the *Hunger for Understanding* workbook. The main aims of this study are to investigate whether the workbook improves understanding of anorexia nervosa, increases motivation to change and enhances the thera-peutic relationship. Findings from this study will be reported in due course.

The *Hunger for Understanding* workbook was initially developed as a thera-peutic tool that could be used by therapists at an inpatient service. Often, the young people who are referred to the service have chronic difficulties with food and weight and have had a diagnosis of anorexia nervosa for some time. They tend to be difficult to engage in treatment and therefore the aim of the workbook was to provide guidance and structure to therapeutic work.

The workbook is based on ideas and techniques that Alison and Sophie have used in therapeutic work, which were influenced by their research and training in this area, and most importantly by talking to patients who have undergone extensive treatment for anorexia nervosa. Their experience of using the workbook to date has been very positive and the feedback received has helped develop and refine the content and structure of the text.

Foreword

Anorexia nervosa can be devastating. It is a destructive disorder that has the unhappy distinction of having the highest mortality rate of all psychiatric conditions. Most people with anorexia nervosa do not die, but their lives – and those of their families – may be blighted for many years, as they struggle to break free from the grip the illness has on them.

The onset of anorexia nervosa most commonly occurs in adolescence and young adulthood. It can develop in children as young as 8 years of age, but more commonly it strikes young people as they negotiate secondary school or college, or at the start of their university or work careers. It develops in young people who invariably have so much potential and so many opportunities ahead of them. Once it has taken hold, it interferes with every aspect of development – physical, emotional, social, academic. It places strains on relationships between family members and with friends. It can mess up education, impair health and fertility, and leave the sufferer feeling confused, distressed and alone, unsure whether their anorexia is a friend or an enemy. While to the onlooker it seems obvious that the person with anorexia nervosa has a serious problem that needs to be dealt with, we know that many sufferers will push away offers of help, often related to their deep-seated fear of putting on weight.

Anorexia nervosa is a disorder that is notoriously difficult to treat. People who have recovered from it often recall feeling very ambivalent and afraid about the process of getting better, which leads them to resist others' attempts to help. However, we know that anorexia can cause real and lasting damage and unhappiness, and in some cases can be fatal. Therapists and clinicians are usually in no doubt that the young person needs help, but often feel at a loss how best to offer this, finding little on their bookshelves by way of guidance and practical suggestions. This is where *Hunger for Understanding* comes in.

Hunger for Understanding is a toolbox of information and practical suggestions for tackling anorexia nervosa in young people, solidly based on theory, research and clinical experience. It has a number of sections covering the purpose and background to the workbook, its theoretical bases, a discussion of common challenges to therapeutic work encountered with these young people, suggestions for skills and techniques to use to overcome these challenges, and guidance on how to work through the chapters that form the workbook itself.

The *Hunger for Understanding* workbook is designed to be used by the therapist and young person together, in a structured and collaborative way, to address some of the key issues that keep the disorder going. It is based on sound psycho-educational principles, with the addition of skills and techniques proven to be helpful, drawn from motivational-enhancement therapy and cognitive-behavioural therapy. The format of the workbook encourages and invites the young person to understand and reflect on their own experience of and response to their anorexia. It contains information, suggests tasks, and prompts the young person to tackle the problematic area of taking real steps to make real changes. This is not a workbook that is only concerned with talking and thinking – there is an important emphasis on doing.

One of the main developmental tasks for all young people is for them to develop an integrated sense of self, which will enable them to achieve an appropriate level of independence from caregivers, take responsibility for themselves and their actions, and make decisions about life choices to enable them to function as adults in society. *Hunger for Understanding* recognises that young people need to learn for themselves, not just by receiving information, but also by trial and error and by reflecting on things in relation to personal experience. Simply telling an adolescent what they should do is unlikely to achieve desired results; they usually need to find things out for themselves. *Hunger for Understanding* sets out to involve the young person directly in the process of recovering from anorexia nervosa. Its accessible format, wealth of practical ideas and reliable information will make it a helpful and valuable addition to the shelves of any therapist who works with young people with eating disorders. More importantly, it seems very well placed to be a helpful and valuable tool in the struggle to help young people leave their anorexia behind for ever.

Rachel Bryant-Waugh
October 2004

Acknowledgements

First, we would like to thank the professionals who suggested submitting this project for publication; without their positive responses to our work, *Hunger for Understanding* would never have come about.

We would also like to express our sincere gratitude to our families and friends for all their support, understanding, encouragement and patience in helping us complete this project.

Thanks also to Rachel Bryant-Waugh for her invaluable knowledge, support and guidance throughout.

Finally, and most importantly, thank you to the young people with whom we have worked for providing us with an insight into their experience and helping us to create *Hunger for Understanding*.

The purpose of the workbook

Therapeutic work with young people with eating disorders can be both extremely challenging and rewarding for professionals. Anorexia nervosa has a devastating impact on the life of the young person and that of their carer(s), but those suffering with it are often reluctant to accept the diagnosis initially and can lack motivation for therapy (Engel and Wilms, 1986). Engaging the young person can be a daunting task for the clinician, and they can struggle to find creative ways and resources to assist them. The *Hunger for Understanding* workbook is designed to provide therapists with a package of practical tools to help them in their work with such young people.

Recent research literature suggests that some form of psychotherapy is essential for most young people with anorexia nervosa, and is more effective than non-specific supportive management by either a psychiatrist or dietician (Palmer and Treasure, 1999). The psychotherapy provided needs to address a range of issues – self-image, self-esteem, developmental, interpersonal and systemic issues and the acquisition of healthier coping strategies (Bell et al., 2000). Several studies have examined the efficacy of cognitive-behavioural therapy (Channon et al., 1989). These studies suggest that individual cognitive-behavioural therapy may be moderately effective in treating this condition, but possibly no more so than other focal therapies. However, Norris (1984) found that this type of therapy was helpful in reducing and managing individual symptoms of the disorder.

Motivational-enhancement therapy has also been found to be useful in the treatment of anorexia nervosa. This therapy focuses on stages of change, with the main goal being to determine which stage the individual is in and then to assist with the movement through the stages to reach the ultimate goal of sustained change. Three studies have applied this model to eating disorder patients (Ward et al., 1996; Blake et al., 1997; Treasure et al., 1999). They concluded that the trans-theoretical model of change provides a useful approach to understanding the process of changing problem behaviours with eating disorders.

Hunger for Understanding incorporates a combination of cognitive-behavioural and motivational-enhancement techniques. There is an important emphasis on tasks to do outside the therapeutic time and it is hoped this will help the young person put into practice in everyday life what is discussed in treatment sessions.

The aim of this approach is to enhance motivation to change through the use of reflective tasks and psycho-education and to provide a structure through which therapists can gradually develop a trusting and collaborative therapeutic relationship. Woven into the workbook are lots of creative ways of exploring the young person's experience, to enable them to think about change, in a way that will help keep both the therapist and the young person engaged in the process.

The illustrations and language used in the workbook are age-appropriate for adolescents with eating disorders and an externalisation model is adopted throughout the workbook. Externalisation is the process whereby the person is separated from the problem. Many people suffering from psychological difficulties often see their difficulties as part of them. This can be a very unhelpful position as it often leaves the person feeling that they have no control over the illness. Helping a young person externalise the illness can help them to make sense of their experience and feel more in control of it, and this is often an important part of the initial recovery process.

▶ Who is *Hunger for Understanding* for?

Hunger for Understanding has been designed for use with young people with anorexia nervosa. While the workbook was written with adolescents aged 11–16 in mind, depending on the ability of the individual, it may be helpful to use this workbook with younger children or young adults.

We know from epidemiological studies that anorexia nervosa tends to have a younger mean age of onset than bulimia nervosa, with two characteristic peak ages of onset – one around puberty, and the other in late adolescence, typically when young people may leave home for the first time. Anorexia nervosa can, however, develop in children before puberty, and also in adults. We have focused on the adolescent age range, as incidence is highest in this age group. There are a number of reasons why this might be, one being that the transition from childhood to adolescence is such an important time in the development of personal identity. At the foundation of self-identity is often a heightened awareness of body image and young people can develop difficulties with sense of self, related body images and body concept (Carr, 1999). When young people are struggling with these concepts, they may be more vulnerable to certain psychological difficulties, such as eating disorders.

Young people of both sexes can develop anorexia and are seen in clinical settings, and although girls outnumber boys, boys do represent a significant minority. In child populations, there appears to be a greater ratio of boys presenting with anorexia, in comparison with adolescent or adult groups. For example, Jacobs and Isaacs (1986) reported a gender ratio of 6:14 (male:female) in pre-pubertal children with anorexia nervosa in comparison to 1:19 in a post-pubertal group. For these reasons *Hunger for Understanding* has been written with both male and female sufferers in mind.

While *Hunger for Understanding* does focus specifically on anorexia nervosa, many of the issues and topics covered are appropriate for young people who display some eating disorder symptoms, such as a significant preoccupation with food, weight and shape and a restricted diet, but have not lost enough weight (15 per cent below normal expected for age and height) to classify them as 'anorexic' (Gowers and Bryant-Waugh, 2004).

The workbook also covers a range of issues making it relevant and appropriate for young people who are being seen on an outpatient or inpatient basis.

▶ Who can use *Hunger for Understanding*?

Hunger for Understanding is intended for use by mental health professionals who work with young people, such as clinical psychologists, psychiatrists, counsellors, occupational therapists and nurses. These professionals are likely to possess the counselling skills that will enable them to contain and explore the emotional effects of working through the material in this workbook.

We have anticipated that such professionals will have some previous experience of working with young people with eating disorders. For those who have not worked with this client group before, we would advise that they supplement their use of this book by familiarising themselves with current research and evidence-based practice in relation to child and adolescent eating disorders. The recommendations made in this book tend to be representative of current national and international thinking. For further information regarding this, please see the following published guidelines: Eating Disorders Association (1994), Royal College of Psychiatrists (2000) and the National Institute of Clinical Excellence (2003).

▶ When and how should *Hunger for Understanding* be used?

Many young people in the early stages of treatment will find the information in the workbook helpful. However, as some sections of the workbook are quite cognitively and emotionally demanding, this type of working style might not be appropriate for a young person in an acute stage of the illness.

The workbook should be administered as part of a treatment package and is not intended as a 'quick answer' to prolonged difficulties. While the workbook was originally designed for individual therapeutic work, it can also be used as part of group work. There are two ways in which this can be approached. Therapists may want to select certain themes and exercises that can then be added to a pre-planned group of exercises. Alternatively, therapists may want to work through the whole workbook to provide a more complete approach.

However, there are several issues that need to be considered when using the workbook as a group approach:

1 Young people suffering from anorexia nervosa may need some preliminary counselling work to prepare them for the group work. This may help them to engage in the work in a more meaningful way.

2 Many of the tasks are demanding and may elicit thoughts and feelings that are difficult to deal with. In these instances, measures such as rules about confidentiality and debrief time should be put in place to ensure that these tasks are suitable for a group format. For many of the tasks, small-group working may be more appropriate, with feedback conducted within the larger group.

3 The workbook contains a lot of information and numerous tasks for the young person to complete. Group facilitators need to review the workbook in conjunction with the needs of their group and plan the sessions accordingly. Within a group format, more discussion may be generated and thus it may be more effective to cover smaller sections of the workbook within the group, leaving other tasks for individual time. As there is a considerable amount of information within the workbook, it may be helpful to develop handouts to support thinking outside of the group format.

4 Group working is a dynamic process and evaluation and feedback can enhance this process. It is important to allow time for this process for both participants and facilitators.

We are very interested in the workbook being used in a group format and would like to hear about people's experience of doing this, both participants and facilitators.

▶ Accessing the workbook electronically

All the workbook resources in this book are available free and in colour to purchasers of the print version. Visit the Wiley website at http://www.wiley.com/go/hunger to find out how to access and download relevant sections of the workbook, which can then be used in clinical sessions with your clients. The materials can be accessed and downloaded as often as required. At the same website, there is an email link through which you can contact the authors of this book and share your comments with them.

► Issues of confidentiality

The workbook should be considered as part of the therapeutic process and issues regarding confidentiality should be explained and negotiated with the young person at the beginning of the work. Issues such as feedback to the wider team of professionals need to be considered and this will vary depending upon the context of the work. It is also essential that therapists consider how feedback will be given to parents and carers and negotiate this with the young person at the outset, taking into account the young person's age. On a more practical level, the therapist and young person should decide where the workbook is kept and whether, for example, the therapist will keep photocopies of the tasks the young person completes for their own files.

Psychological interventions for anorexia nervosa and the role of psycho-education

Research suggests that eating disorders have the highest mortality rate of all psychological problems. For this reason alone, the development of prevention and effective treatment programmes is an important priority for healthcare professionals (Szmukler and Dare, 1991). Many different pharmacological, psychological and physical interventions have been developed and used for the treatment of anorexia nervosa.

When considering any treatment option, it is important to clarify the treatment aims and objectives. The American Psychiatric Association (1999a) suggests the following as key treatment goals:

- correction of the biological and psychological sequelae of malnutrition, including weight restoration;
- prevention or correction of any nutritional complications that have arisen from starvation;
- restoration of normal eating pattern, including normal perceptions of hunger and satiety;
- reduction of bingeing and purging;
- promotion of patient understanding regarding the disorder and the associated symptoms;
- change in the behaviours and dysfunctional attitudes that relate to the eating disorder;
- improvements in intrapersonal and interpersonal functioning;
- restoration of normal exercise pattern;
- attention to any co-morbid psychopathology and psychological conflicts that reinforce or maintain eating disorder behaviour.

The American Psychiatric Association (APA) recommends a pre-treatment evaluation for each patient, to determine the appropriate treatment goals. They suggest that such an evaluation should include assessment of medical complications, suicidality, body weight, motivation to recover, co-morbid disorders, structure needed for eating and weight gain, self-care ability, purging behaviour, environmental stress and treatment availability (APA, 1999b).

▶ Psychological interventions

To date, the literature is unclear as to which type of psychological intervention for anorexia nervosa is most effective, because there is insufficient research evidence upon which to base anything other than general recommendations. There have been some studies that have evaluated different treatment approaches, for example, cognitive-behavioural therapy (Norris, 1984; Channon et al., 1989), cognitive analytic therapy (Treasure et al., 1995; Dare et al., 2001), interpersonal therapy (Klerman et al., 1984) and family therapy (Russell et al., 1987; Le Grange et al., 1992; Eilser et al., 1997; Wilson and Fairburn, 1998). While some of this research has been conducted within child and adolescent populations, there is still a growing demand for more research evaluating the different approaches. The National Institute of Clinical Excellence (2004) found insufficient evidence to conclude that any particular specialist psychotherapy is superior to others in the treatment of adults with anorexia nervosa, either at the end of treatment or by follow-up. This report also suggested that there was insufficient evidence to conclude that any one type of psychotherapy was more acceptable to patients than others.

In our experience, individual psychotherapeutic management that provides empathetic understanding, praise of positive efforts, coaching and other positive behavioural reinforcement is beneficial, especially after malnutrition is corrected and weight gain has begun. In our work with young people with anorexia nervosa, we have drawn on three therapeutic approaches in particular, these are motivational-enhancement therapy (MET), cognitive-behavioural therapy (CBT) and psycho-education. MET acknowledges the individual's current state of motivation to change and uses specific therapeutic techniques to enhance intrinsic motivation by developing a discrepancy between present behaviour and broader life goals. CBT aims to reduce psychological distress by altering thought processes, and psycho-education (aimed at helping people understand more about their difficulties) is a central component of CBT.

We believe the combination of these approaches can help the young person make sense of the confusing and distressing experience of anorexia nervosa. If people can understand their difficulties, they can then be equipped with skills to protect themselves from further decline and are more likely to be motivated to aim for change in their life. These are active therapies that are appropriate for working with child and adolescent populations and encourage young people to become a collaborative partner in the therapy.

Motivational-enhancement therapy (MET)

Motivational-enhancement therapy is derived from integrating the transtheoretical model of change with the skills of motivational interviewing. The goal of the therapy is to determine which stage the individual is in and then to assist with the movement through the stages to reach the ultimate goal of sustained change.

The therapy is based on the trans-theoretical model of change (Prochaska and DiClemente, 1992). This model of change was developed in the addictions field in an attempt to understand how people change unwanted behaviours. The model describes five stages through which people pass while trying to change. Each stage represents a motivational level of change (see Table 2.1).

This model of change views the stages of change as a cycle as opposed to a linear progression (see p. 100 in the workbook). Individuals often have to go through the stages more than once before the problem behaviour is eliminated.

Motivational interviewing is a therapeutic style that was also developed in the field of addictions (Miller and Rollnick, 1991). The goal of motivational interviewing is to help clients reach a decision to change by increasing intrinsic motivation. This is accomplished by helping clients to recognise the discrepancy between their present behaviour and their broader life goals or values.

Three studies have applied this model to eating disorder patients (Ward et al., 1996; Blake et al., 1997; Treasure et al., 1999). They concluded that the

Table 2.1 The stages of change model

Stages	Behaviour
Pre-contemplation	The behaviour is not recognised as a problem and there is no effort to change
Contemplation	There is recognition of the problem behaviour but ambivalence about whether or not to change
Preparation	The individual wants to change his/her behaviour but does not know how to or needs assistance
Action	The individual is in the process of changing the behaviour
Maintenance	The individual maintains the change in behaviour and avoids regression to the problem behaviour

Source: Data from Prochaska and DiClemente (1992)

trans-theoretical model of change provides a useful approach to understanding the process of changing problem behaviours with eating disorders. Further research in these areas is currently ongoing.

Cognitive-behavioural therapy (CBT)

CBT is an active therapy to help people recognise and modify dysfunctional thoughts about their current life situation and beliefs about themselves and their world. The underlying assumption of CBT is that behaviours, thoughts and feelings are learned through life experiences, and can therefore be unlearned or modified. The patient is encouraged through the use of reflective tasks to make links between thoughts and their subsequent feelings and behaviour.

Unlike many other therapies, CBT encourages therapists to educate the patient about their problems and this is teamed with the role of listener. Such features of the work encourage a collaborative relationship as the therapist and patient work together to solve the patient's problems. Hilde Bruch, who is well known for her work with people with eating disorders, believed that work in this area has to be collaborative in order to be effective.

The CBT approach as applied to eating disorders involves treating the symptoms of weight loss and dieting in a behavioural way, building on coping skills, addressing misconceptions about weight, shape and food and cognitively treating dysfunctional beliefs about shape, weight and low self-esteem. There is also an emphasis on enhancing interpersonal skills and addressing family issues, such as communication.

Because of the collaborative nature of CBT work, there is a continuous process of checking back with the patient to clarify their views and monitor their motivation to change. This approach is clearly very useful when working with anorexia nervosa where problems of motivation are almost intrinsic to the therapeutic work.

CBT is widely used with a range of psychological problems in child and adolescent services and reviews indicate promising results (Wallace et al., 1995; Roth and Fonagy, 1996; Kazdin and Weisz, 1998). With regards to research in anorexia nervosa, although there has been little research conducted, indications are that CBT is equally as effective as other focal therapies, but may be particularly helpful in reducing and managing specific symptoms of the disorder, for example, reducing body image disturbance (Norris, 1984).

Professionals who are unfamiliar with CBT work may benefit from reading Paul Stallard's *Think Good – Feel Good* (2002), which is a CBT workbook for young people covering a range of psychological problems. Another useful text that specifically applies CBT to anorexia nervosa is Christopher Freeman's

Overcoming Anorexia Nervosa: A Self-help Guide Using Cognitive-behavioural Techniques (2002).

▶ Psycho-education in anorexia nervosa

Unfortunately many professionals struggle to engage people with anorexia and a high proportion drop-out of treatment prematurely. If professionals can enable the individual to feel in control of their treatment and work in a collaborative manner, they may be more willing to engage in the very arduous task of overcoming anorexia nervosa (Eivors et al., 2003).

There have been relatively few studies that have attempted to elicit patients' views on their treatment experience and what they found helpful or unhelpful. However, this kind of research can greatly benefit clinical practice and help clinicians develop treatments which are not only effective but are mindful of the patients' wishes.

Hsu et al. (1992) attempted to discover which factors facilitated recovery. Personality strength, self-confidence, being understood and being ready were cited as important. Le Grange and Gelman (1998) elicited the views of patients (suffering with both anorexia and bulimia nervosa) on treatment. They identified psycho-education, a supportive environment, challenging dysfunctional beliefs and behavioural strategies as helpful components of treatment. Many, however, felt the causes of their problems were inadequately dealt with in treatment.

Eivors et al. (2003) explored the treatment experiences of eight women in a qualitative study investigating reasons for drop-out. The women highlighted the very 'functional' nature of anorexia nervosa in helping them regain a sense of control over their world. However, their interactions with others (including professionals) often resulted in attempts to deal with the symptoms of starvation without addressing the underlying meaning. This recreates a sense of lost control that initially precipitated the onset of their eating difficulties and resulted in the women prematurely ending treatment. All too often the reasons behind actions are neglected in favour of controlling and containing the behaviour.

Such research clearly indicates that patients need to feel in control of their treatment. The women in the study by Eivors et al. (2003) had clear ideas regarding the kind of approach they believed they would have benefited from. Broadly speaking, what they were hoping for in treatment was insight and understanding.

Such insights into the patients' experience of treatment for anorexia nervosa can provide us with extremely useful information as to how we might best approach therapy. Patients are asking for a supportive and collaborative relationship in which they can make sense of their difficulties, challenge their unhelpful beliefs and develop strategies to overcome their difficulties. It is for these reasons that the *Hunger for Understanding* workbook has been developed.

As we have already described, research indicates that motivational-enhancement work and cognitive-behavioural therapy have a very useful role in the treatment of eating disorders. Psycho-education is a central part of both approaches. For example, it is sometimes easy to assume that people with anorexia nervosa have a good knowledge of dieting and weight. However, despite the amount of time and energy devoted to this subject, many have faulty beliefs and assumptions about food, weight and shape that can maintain extreme dieting behaviour.

The key issues covered through psycho-education in anorexia nervosa have been incorporated into the *Hunger for Understanding* workbook. They are as follows.

The psychological symptoms of starvation

Frequently, anorectic patients misinterpret their preoccupation with food, fluctuating moods, urges to binge, cognitive impairment and social withdrawal as secondary to their attempts to control their weight (Garner et al., 1997). It is useful for the therapist to re-attribute them to dieting and/or starvation as this can relieve some of the guilt and shame that the patient often attributes to an individual flaw.

The cultural context of eating disorders

Environments have a powerful influence in predisposing some young people to dieting and subsequent eating disorders. Frequently, these powerful messages (from a variety of sources, e.g. the media, peers, family) are readily assimilated into the young person's belief system and are accepted as 'truths', for example, you have to be less than x pounds in order to be successful. Understanding, recognising and challenging the insidious impact of these messages are extremely helpful for young people.

Set-point theory

Studies indicate that body weight is regulated to maintain a stable weight and resist losing or increasing weight (Keesey, 1993). When the body loses or increases weight, the metabolism adjusts to ensure that the body returns to its stable point. The Keys et al. (1950) study challenges the popular notion that weight is easily altered if people possess the necessary 'will power' and also demonstrates the enormous cognitive, physical and emotional impact of starvation.

The physical effects of starvation

The physiological effects of both starvation and associated behaviours (e.g. bingeing, laxative use, etc.) can have a devastating impact on development and potentially can be life-threatening. It is important that sufferers are informed about the potential effects of starvation and the complications that can occur. When this information is presented as fact rather than threats, it can help the person to take responsibility for managing their behaviour and reduce the potential risks associated with anorexia nervosa.

Therapeutic challenges, skills and techniques

▶ Challenges of work with people with anorexia nervosa

There are a number of difficulties specific to this area of work that professionals can expect to face. Frequently, professionals can feel overwhelmed in their task and a sense of hopelessness can pervade the therapeutic relationship. It is important first to recognise the complex nature of this work. Eating disorders seem to be caused by a number of factors and it is not surprising, then, that successful treatment will require the skills and expertise of many different professionals who can work as a team.

The main tasks of treatment can crudely be divided into the physical and psychological aspects, although clearly there is often a great deal of overlap between the two.

Physical issues

In adults, recovery involves returning to the individual's pre-morbid physical state, whereas in adolescence there are no such clear markers to gauge recovery by. Because of the rapid growth that occurs at this time, weight targets will require close monitoring and constant revision by physicians who understand normal adolescent growth and development (Gowers and Bryant-Waugh, 2004).

Parents will also need to be involved in monitoring the young person's food intake and physical well-being. They may also benefit from psycho-education material to help them assess relevant signs and symptoms.

Due to potential medical complications that can occur in this age group, Kreipe et al. (1995) have suggested that the threshold for medical intervention in adolescents should be lower than in adults. It is therefore advisable to make links with the next tier of intervention at an early stage, whether this is with a specialist eating disorder team or inpatient unit.

Psychological issues

Although current research regarding the efficacy of specific therapeutic treatments is inconclusive, a therapeutic relationship that can be sustained throughout the duration of the disorder is essential (Ebeling et al., 2003). Regardless of the type of therapy offered, the aim should be to offer the young person the opportunity to make sense of their experience and develop age-appropriate ways of coping. The pace, timing and nature of the therapeutic work should at all times reflect the individual's developmental age. It is important to be mindful of the enormous changes that occur between the ages of 11–16 and issues such as consent, confidentiality and the degree of involvement of carers will vary considerably.

Shame, denial and lack of insight are common features of anorexia nervosa. Eating disorders such as anorexia nervosa can also be extremely 'functional' and there are many secondary gains (such as providing a sense of direction, achievement and identity). All such issues present significant challenges to therapists in building and maintaining an open, honest and trusting relationship. It is therefore important for therapists to identify and attribute these issues to anorexia nervosa and not to the individual. It is also vital that therapists have access to regular supervision in order to contain the anxieties and frustrations that will inevitably arise out of such work. Despite these challenges it is possible to develop and maintain a positive therapeutic relationship with young people suffering from anorexia nervosa.

The young person will require clear and concise explanations regarding their treatment. Where possible, it is advisable to forewarn them about potential changes, as this will enhance their sense of control over the treatment process. It is also important to discuss from the outset the boundaries of confidentiality.

Consistency is also essential for the same reason. For example, there should be an agreement regarding who weighs the young person and how often, when and how parents are involved in sessions and, as much as possible, consistency with regards to the location and timing of appointments.

Boundaries and limit setting are of particular importance. Recovery is often slow and in some instances the patient may demonstrate manipulative behaviours in an attempt to cope with unmet needs. They may deny they have a problem, refuse treatment or feign compliance. It is important to recognise these behaviours and manage them with clear, concise and consistent responses among the team of professionals working with the individual. There must be clear and regular communication between all those involved in the treatment process. This means open channels of communication between professionals (who may not always be working in the same location) and also within the family (e.g. between parents).

Therapists should be mindful of their own relationship with food and weight and consider how these may be inadvertently communicated to the patient. It is well known that clients tend to adopt the personal values of their therapists during the course of successful psychotherapy (Beutler et al., 1994), and therefore one's own issues in relation to key concepts such as perfectionism, self-control, emotional expression, assertiveness and self-acceptance are of the utmost importance. It is important to assess for other psychological issues that the young person may also need help with, such as low self-esteem, anxiety, depression, deliberate self-harm and obsessional compulsive disorder.

The therapist should be vigilant to the patient's fluctuations in their motivation to change and adapt their therapeutic style and goals accordingly. This will enable the therapist and patient to maintain a positive therapeutic alliance and may help to protect against a sense of hopelessness. It is important to acknowledge the individual's struggle, as any intervention is likely to cause extreme anxiety. In most cases therapists are asking the young person to do the things they fear most.

▶ Therapeutic skills and techniques

There are a number of useful therapeutic techniques, which may be useful with this client group, as shown below.

Externalisation

Externalisation is an attempt to separate the person and the problem. This technique seems particularly useful when working with young people with anorexia as all too often the disorder can become their identity.

Instilling hope

Many young people suffering from eating disorders and particularly anorexia nervosa have little confidence in their ability to change and get better. The aim of the workbook is to enhance insight and motivation to change. Until the young person is sufficiently motivated to change, the therapist can have an important role in holding and maintaining a sense of hope. The role may be equated to that of a 'cheerleader'. Identifying exceptions and even the smallest steps towards change can have an extremely powerful effect in instilling a sense of hope. A belief in the young person's ability to change can create a positive self-fulfilling prophecy.

Empathy

Research consistently highlights that empathy can be a significant determinant of a patient's response to treatment (Luborsky et al., 1985). It has also been demonstrated that confrontational counselling has been associated with a high drop-out rate and poor outcome (Miller, 1983). Therefore qualities such as warmth, sensitivity, compassion, honesty, flexibility, genuineness, acceptance and positive regard will all greatly enhance the therapeutic alliance and ultimately the outcome.

Developing emotional awareness

Bruch (1962, 1973) suggested that the inability to accurately identify and respond to emotions was fundamental to anorexia nervosa. This often leads patients to a mistrust of their own motives, behaviours and thoughts and results in exaggerated self-monitoring and rigidity. This may be articulated by patients as a denial of anger, for example. The therapist has an important role in helping the patient first of all to develop an emotional vocabulary (e.g. keeping a diary of emotions, or watching their favourite soap opera and identifying the emotional states of the characters), and then linking their emotions and actions.

Rolling with resistance

Miller and Rollnick (2002) suggest a good principle is to respond to resistance with non-resistance. Acknowledging the individual's disagreement, feeling or perception then allows a greater opportunity to explore with the person, rather than take opposing sides, which is likely to result in a therapeutic impasse.

Dealing with distress

Many of the issues covered in this workbook may cause the young person distress. As discussed above, this work should take place within the context of a therapeutic relationship. Within this context a professional should support the young person with an awareness of mental health issues for young people.

In order to help the young person gain a sense of control and ownership over the workbook, it is essential that the therapist works at a pace that is comfortable and appropriate for the individual.

Managing relapses

It is useful for the therapist to prepare the patient for potential relapses, especially those who binge and purge at stressful times. Often the patient will believe that one episode of bingeing means there is no hope of recovery and that all is lost. The therapist can help the patient to reframe the relapse and move on from perfectionist and dichotomous thinking by encouraging the patient to practise the 4 Rs (Garner et al., 1997):

Reframe the episode as a 'slip', and not as a full-blown disaster.

Renew the commitment to long-term recovery.

Return to the plan of regular eating without compensatory activities such as over-exercising.

Re-institute behavioural controls (e.g. distraction) to interrupt future episodes.

◄ CHAPTER FOUR ►

The contents of the workbook and guidelines for use

There are 11 sections in the workbook, starting with a general introduction outlining the aims and objectives of the book. Each chapter begins by offering the young person an overview of the information and theory available on the topic, before asking them to complete a number of related tasks.

The workbook has been designed so that it can be used flexibly by therapists who may need to take into consideration factors such as their own and the patient's time constraints, the intellectual and developmental level of the patient, and the context of therapy, i.e. group or individual, outpatient or inpatient.

The young person and therapist would normally start the workbook by reading through the material together. Once the therapist feels confident that the young person understands the rationale of the approach and the format of the workbook, they could then introduce the idea of reading chapters outside of the sessions. Likewise, it may be appropriate to begin thinking about tasks within the session, but ask the young person to continue to work on them in the following week. If the workbook is used within a group setting, the members could be given chapters to read and then complete tasks interactively within the group.

Here we describe each section by first offering a brief synopsis of the theoretical background and then giving more detailed suggestions for ways of working through the sections and descriptions of the various tasks.

► Section 1 What is anorexia nervosa?

This is a comprehensive section defining anorexia nervosa for the young person and encouraging them to start to think about the signs and symptoms and the possible causes.

People suffering with anorexia nervosa are sometimes classified into 'restricting types' or 'binge/purging types' (i.e. those who keep their weight down solely by restricting their food, and those who binge and purge by making themselves vomit or by taking laxatives, diuretics or enemas). However, there are a number of common features in both groups. They both will have an intense fear of gaining weight and will attempt to restrict their food intake. Frequently, sufferers will use strenuous exercise to burn off calories, and they may also take a keen interest in cookery, although they will avoid eating the food they make.

There may also be noticeable changes in personality, such as increasing seriousness and introversion. Young people suffering from anorexia nervosa may become less outgoing and fun. Other common features of anorexia nervosa are perfectionism, obsessive-compulsive behaviour, poor self-image and mood disturbance. A number of young people may also self-harm. Contact with friends and outside interests may reduce considerably and be replaced by an obsessional interest in food. Parents often find that this type of behaviour has an increasingly controlling impact on the family.

Tasks in Section 1

Task 1.1, 'Naming anorexia', asks the young person to do just that. It is hoped that by naming their anorexia, it will help the young person to think about anorexia as external to them while also enabling them to personalise their experience.

Task 1.2, 'Similarities and differences', encourages the young person to consider the similarities and differences in their experience compared to other sufferers. Denial of anorexia nervosa is a common feature of the disorder and the aim of this task is to encourage the young person to share and label some of the defences they hold that may be preventing them from acknowledging their difficulties.

The final task in this section, 'What does anorexia look like?', is more creative and asks the young person to draw a picture of their anorexia. Again, the aim is to help the person think about the individual meaning of their difficulties, while also encouraging them to gain a sense of control over the experience. Visualising anorexia using an image can help to achieve this. An alternative task might be to construct a model of anorexia using clay or craft materials.

▶ Section 2 What causes anorexia?

The second section focuses in more detail on the causes of anorexia nervosa. This involves discussion of various factors that may contribute to the development of the illness such as genetic factors, environmental factors, family factors and personality factors. Knowledge about the causes of anorexia nervosa is inconclusive, and the causes may be varied. As this is a complex area, we will give a brief overview here of the research carried out into the personalities, genetics, environments and biochemistry of people who are affected.

Bruch (1973) outlined three areas of psychological concern in anorexia nervosa. These were:

1 a distorted body image;

2 an inaccurate perception of internal states;

3 a paralysing sense of ineffectiveness.

Perceived control, low self-esteem and self-directed hostility are also factors thought to characterise anorectic patients (Williams et al., 1993).

Eating disorders also tend to run in families, with female relatives most often affected. For instance, a girl has a 10–20 times higher risk of developing anorexia nervosa if she has a sibling with the disorder. This suggests that genetic factors may predispose some people to eating disorders. Behavioural and environmental influences may also play a role. Stressful events are likely to increase the risk of eating disorders as well.

Traumatic events, such as being a victim of sexual abuse, the loss of a parent at a very young age, parents being absent for long periods of time during childhood or a serious illness in a close relative or friend, are also known to predispose anorexia. Events or circumstances causing intense distress in the child are factors suspected of increasing vulnerability to anorexia.

Some suggest that family factors may play a role in the development of eating disorders. Families of anorectic patients are generally considered much more homogenetic than other families and are often characterised as rigid, overprotecting, conflict-avoiding and discouraging of individuality (Minuchin et al., 1978). There may be a focus on performance and an intense involvement in the child's life by one or both parents. Families who operate in very rigid, rule-governed ways may also feel threatened by the transition of adolescence (Palazzoli, 1978). However, it is extremely difficult to establish whether dysfunctional interaction within families is a cause or consequence of anorexia.

Crisp (1997) believed anorexia nervosa was due to an avoidance of the physical and psychological challenges of puberty. The avoidance involves pursuing and maintaining a weight that is sub-pubertal (usually under 95–100 pounds). Because weight is so unstable and the body's need to grow and ingest food is so powerful, further weight loss may be necessary to ensure that the individual does not cross the threshold that would take them into puberty.

In studies of the biochemical functions of people with eating disorders, scientists have found that the neurotransmitters serotonin and norepinephrine are decreased in those with anorexia, which links them with patients suffering from depression. People with anorexia nervosa also tend to have higher than normal levels of cortisol (a brain hormone released in response to stress) and vasopressin (a brain chemical found to be abnormal in patients with obsessive-compulsive disorder).

Given that anorexia nervosa seems to be predominantly confined to women and in Western societies, many researchers have raised questions regarding cultural influences in predisposing young women to dieting and ultimately anorexia nervosa. Herzog et al. (1984) suggest that in contexts where there is an emphasis on physical appearance and size and weight are significant (e.g. ballet dancers, models and jockeys), both men and women are susceptible to conform to society's slim ideal.

There seems to be some consensus that anorexia nervosa is determined multifactorally by a combination of biological, social and psychological factors (Garner et al., 1982).

Tasks in Section 2

Task 2.1, 'Factors that contribute to the development of anorexia', encourages the young person to think about the common myths, which can then be explored and clarified. An additional task might be to encourage the young person to look through magazines and newspapers and bring in interesting articles to discuss, or in younger children, make a collage.

The second task, 'Life experiences', is more reflective and aimed at a personal level, thinking about life experiences and the impact on body image. Again, the individual could bring in photographs of themself to encourage recollection of different events, people and experiences and reflect on how they have felt about themselves at different times.

At the end of this section, the young person is asked to reflect on their own thoughts and create a 'narrative' regarding how they feel anorexia developed for them. The aim of 'Your story' is to help the individual make sense and give meaning to some very confusing experiences. The timeline is a more structured way of exploring this and can help widen the discussion regarding the onset of anorexia from weight and food to other transitions. It is particularly important here to spend time thinking about the psychological and physical challenges of adolescence, whether these are past, current or anticipated.

For example, the establishment of a clear sense of identity is one of the major tasks of adolescence. At the foundation of adolescent self-awareness, the 'self-image' is a representation of the body: what it is like and how it looks to others. This self-perception can be strongly influenced by cultural and societal norms. The importance of body image to our culture as a whole is obvious in terms of the widespread expenditure of time and effort that is given to the body's appearance.

▶ Section 3 How does dieting affect us?

The third section of the workbook aims to provide education about the effects of dieting. For many young people, dieting may have been the first step into developing eating difficulties. Information about what happens to our bodies when we diet is provided. This includes descriptions of experiments that have been conducted to investigate the effects of dieting. A brief overview of the 'set-point' theory of dieting is given with a case example detailing specific weight loss and the physiological effects of this. Also, a detailed description of the Keys study (1950) is provided. This aims to demonstrate the effects of food restriction and the impact this has on thoughts, feelings and behaviours. Findings from the Keys experiment are then likened to the modern-day symptoms of eating disorders. This section may normalise some of the psychological symptoms of dieting and help the young person to see how many of the effects of anorexia nervosa are maintained by dieting.

Tasks in Section 3

The tasks in this section ask the young person to think about his or her own eating patterns. 'Anorexia's choice', 'A typical meal before anorexia', 'A healthy choice' and 'Compare the plates!' aim to help the young person think about what normal eating was before anorexia and how this may have been distorted by the development of the illness. It is important to be aware that the individual may attempt to mask the true extent of their difficulties by distorting or denying their current food intake. Rather than challenging this directly, it may be helpful to depersonalise this task initially, by asking them to think about what someone else with anorexia is likely to manage to eat. Equally, they may find it difficult to consider what a normal, healthy meal is. It may be useful to encourage the person to think about the different food requirements of people they know, such as friends, children, adults, etc. They could spend time just observing others eat and then come back to these tasks.

Finally, Task 3.5, 'Good and bad food', is given as frequently young people divide foods into these dichotomous categories, which prevents them from losing control over food. This could be a creative task, either drawing the food, or cutting out pictures from magazines. It is important to add humour (obviously where appropriate) to the tasks, so that the young person can be freed from the rigidity that anorexia places on their world. It may also be helpful to explore when and how these distinctions developed.

▶ Section 4 How does anorexia affect you?

The fourth section deals with the effects of anorexia, focusing on changes in perception, in feelings, in behaviour, and physical changes. This chapter aims to outline the changes in such a way that they can be easily recognised by someone who has anorexia nervosa. Changes in the way we see our bodies are outlined with concrete examples given. This is followed by changes in feelings experienced and subsequent changes in behaviour. There is a detailed section on the physiological effects of anorexia nervosa that provides clear descriptions of some of the physical problems associated with the disorder. Information on how these changes may also impact on family and friends is also included.

Tasks in Section 4

Task 4.1, 'Anorexia's body image', concludes this section, where the young person is asked to think about their own body image and how they perceive their body at the present time. In Task 4.2, 'Other people's image', the young person is asked to think about how other people may see them and in Task 4.3, 'Comparing images', to think about the differences between these two perceptions.

The last task in this section, 'The losses from having anorexia', encourages the young person to think about what anorexia may have deprived them of, by labelling the 'losses'. This is a creative task where the losses are drawn or written on to gravestones or coffins. This can be a very powerful and overwhelming task and it is important to allow the young person time to acknowledge and grieve for the losses. However, it may also be relevant to explore which ones are permanent and which ones are temporary as a result of transition, change or the anorexia, and how the situation might be different in the future.

▶ Section 5 What keeps anorexia going?

The fifth section focuses on the maintenance factors involved in anorexia. This involves a description of some of the cognitive traps that young people may fall into. Understanding more about the factors maintaining anorexia nervosa is a key part of the recovery process. This understanding is key for the individual and also for family and friends who may have become part of the maintenance cycle. This section aims to explain more about maintenance using examples that can be recognised by young people experiencing anorexia nervosa.

Tasks in Section 5

In Task 5.1, 'What keeps anorexia going for you?', the young person is asked to draw on their own experiences and think about what sustains anorexia in their own circumstances. The aim of the 'Closeness circles' task is to help the young person recognise important relationships in their life and consider how anorexia may have impacted upon them. If there is a discrepancy between the position of a person in the two drawings (e.g. a family member is placed as being very close in the first circle, when ideally they would like some space), this can then be explored by the therapist in more detail, giving consideration to how the absence and/or presence of anorexia may impact on this goal.

▶ Section 6 The tricks anorexia plays

In this section, both physical and psychological factors are explored and referred to as 'traps'. The analogy of anorexia as a bully or a friend acknowledges the functional/helpful aspects of the disorder and again reinforces the externalisation process.

Tasks in Section 6

The externalisation of anorexia is encouraged further in the tasks at the end of Section 6, 'How clever is your anorexia?', 'My best mate', 'The bully' and 'The future', in which the young person is asked to consider the messages anorexia gives them about life with or without the illness.

Externalisation of anorexia in this way can help the young person gain a sense of control over their experiences and may help them to re-attribute their difficulties to anorexia, rather than dispositional weaknesses. The therapist can further expand this task to consider how the 'best mate' and 'bully' might impact on the therapeutic relationship. For example, 'If the bully was sitting on your shoulder right now, what would it be saying about you using the workbook?', or 'How might the best friend fool me when we are working through this?' Circular questioning would also work well here, for example, asking the young person what their mother, father, siblings, friends have noticed about the tricks anorexia plays.

Expanding on 'The future' task, therapists might also encourage the young person to imagine meeting a friend in one year's time, five years' time and ten years' time with and without anorexia. This can help the young person consider the long-term effects of the illness and highlight how much of life they are likely to miss out on. This could be role-played with the therapist taking on the part of the friend.

▶ Section 7 Thinking about change

Many sufferers feel overwhelmed by the thought of working towards recovery and are unsure of what this may involve. Section 7 attempts to normalise feelings of ambivalence and demystify the process of recovery. This section includes actual quotes from sufferers that clearly portray the emotional turmoil of contemplating change and real-life experiences of overcoming this disorder.

It outlines the important stages within this recovery process using the Prochaska and DiClemente stages of change model (1992). This model of change is beneficial to the therapeutic process in a number of ways. It can provide the therapist and patient with a shared understanding of the current state of motivation for that individual. By labelling this, they can then acknowledge and normalise fluctuations in motivation. The therapist's awareness of these stages can help direct the treatment process by ensuring that there is a 'fit' between the therapeutic style and the individual's motivation to change. For example, in the pre-contemplation stage, the patient is unlikely to respond to advice to increase their food intake, but they may benefit from tasks centred on recognising their difficulties.

Tasks in Section 7

Tasks 7.1, 'How anorexia helps', and 7.2, 'How anorexia hinders', are particularly useful at the contemplation stage. We would envisage that most young people having worked through the workbook to this point would be at the contemplation stage or even the action stage. These tasks can help shift the decisional balance and encourage the young person to consider making change. It is important for the young person to spend time considering the useful aspects of the disorder and acknowledge how functional it may have been in their life. In doing so, the therapist is helping the young person to accept the loss of this coping strategy. This is further acknowledged by writing a 'Farewell letter' to anorexia. It may be important for the young person to do something symbolic with the farewell letter, such as burying it, burning it or keeping it locked away somewhere.

Once the young person has made their lists of how anorexia helps and hinders, they might be encouraged by the therapist to test out some of their assumptions. For example, if the young person believes anorexia helps him/her feel better about him/herself, they could turn the statement into a question and try an experiment, such as keeping a mood chart throughout the week.

Task 7.4, 'Where are you?', helps the young person to recognise their position within the cycle of change and to acknowledge fluctuations in their motivation by identifying times when they have been at different stages within the cycle. Therapists are encouraged to help the young person consider how small steps might help enhance their motivation.

Tasks 7.5, 'Importance of change', and 7.7, 'Level of confidence', both help the young person and therapist to identify what issues may underlie motivation. For example, if an individual rates change as important, but confidence as low, then the therapist can focus their efforts on enhancing confidence by tasks such as 'Challenges I've faced before'. Alternatively, a patient who rates importance of change as low could be encouraged to consider the short-term and long-term benefits of overcoming anorexia in Task 7.6, 'Reasons for change'.

▶ Section 8 Getting better

This section is aimed at creating cognitive and behavioural change and therefore has more tasks for the young person to complete than any other section of the workbook. It is essential that the therapist works through this section at an appropriate pace that is individualised to the young person's needs.

Tasks in Section 8

There are many tasks based on standard cognitive-behavioural and motivational-enhancement techniques within this section that encourage the young person to think about the resources they have within themselves and around them. Task 8.2, 'Rules for living that you have in your life', asks the young person about the dysfunctional assumptions they hold. Once recognised, the young person can be encouraged to consider how these rules impact on their emotions, thoughts and behaviour. Task 8.3, 'How others can help or hinder', looks at the roles other key people play and can help the young person communicate their needs to others around them.

Task 8.4, 'My anorexia-free time', encourages the young person to challenge dysfunctional assumptions through behavioural experiments, for example, trying a small amount of foods that the young person may deem to be 'unsafe', or giving an opinion when asked. Task 8.5, 'Fishing for thoughts', helps the young person identify unhelpful thoughts, while Tasks 8.6 and 8.7, 'What would my best friend say?' and 'Be your own agony aunt', encourage them to distance themselves from the thoughts and begin to challenge them.

Next, the young person is asked to make a list under the heading, 'When anorexia is no longer in control, I will . . .' This exercise aims to focus the young person on recovery and life without anorexia. Task 8.9, 'Taking care of myself', is important preparation for the recovery stage and Task 8.10, 'A reminder to myself', introduces a tool that will be useful to the young person when they experience setbacks. Finally, in 'How can I help myself?', the young person is asked to fill a suitcase with things that will help them through the recovery journey.

It is particularly important to allow time to reflect on the tasks attempted. The therapist will also need to be aware of resistance to trying out alternatives at this stage where there is more of a behavioural focus on change. If you have reached this point and the young person appears very reluctant to attempt the tasks, it is important to explore this directly, and maybe work back through some of the earlier sections, possibly identifying with their current stage of readiness to change using the information in the 'Thinking about change' section (p. 93).

▶ Section 9 Teamwork

This section helps guide the young person through the daunting task of recovery by explaining the importance of teamwork, highlighting the physical and psychological aspects of recovery and the role of professionals who may be involved in the young person's care. It also encourages the young person to consider themselves and their family as part of the treatment team so that they will feel integral to the recovery process. This section explains in some detail the likely demands of treatment, such as re-feeding, as it is very important that both the patient and the family understand the treatment rationale. This will help allay the inevitable anxieties for both when the process begins.

Task in Section 9

Reading through this section may have raised some questions or anxieties and the task, 'My team', is therefore about identifying existing support (both formal and informal) and encouraging the young person to consider how each person may help them address their anxieties and treatment goals.

▶ Section 10 Becoming assertive

Section 10 focuses specifically on assertiveness and encourages the young person to identify different types of communication. The aim is to help the young person recognise their rights as being equal to others and develop skills to help them express feelings and opinions in an open and direct way, rather than using starvation as a form of communication.

Tasks in Section 10

'What is assertiveness?' The young person answers this question at the start and the end of this section so that any misconceptions about assertiveness can be identified and challenged. This section is very interactive, as the young person is asked to reflect on their likely reaction in different scenarios in Task 10.2, 'What would you do?', and identify examples of assertive, passive and aggressive behaviour. Task 10.3, 'Review your rights', can help the young person identify dysfunctional assumptions about themselves and consider how such beliefs may have developed. The final task, 'Pocket-size rights', asks the young person to keep their human rights safe by carrying around with them a card with their rights on as a tangible reminder. This will hopefully encourage them to experiment with assertiveness skills and enable them to reflect on the experience of protecting their rights.

At this point, the therapist can integrate a number of the cognitive-behavioural techniques outlined in Section 8, 'Getting better', such as fishing for healthy assertive thoughts or thinking about an issue from a friend's perspective. The therapist can also encourage the young person to utilise assertiveness skills within the context of the therapeutic relationship, by encouraging the young person to make choices about the therapy where appropriate.

▶ Section 11 Myths and questions about anorexia nervosa

This section of the workbook hopes to serve to dispel some of the myths regarding anorexia, replacing incorrect information with factual information. Task 11.1, 'Your own questions', encourages the young person to actively think about any questions they may have regarding anorexia.

▶ Some good advice and messages of support

The final part of the workbook aims to offer motivation and encouragement by presenting messages from young people who have suffered and recovered from anorexia nervosa. These messages of support may motivate the young person in their battle and provide real proof that it is possible.

The final task, 'Write your own message of inspiration', encourages the young person to write their own inspirational message. This can be used to help to motivate them or to help motivate other young people experiencing similar difficulties. We would encourage both the therapist and young person to write a letter to each other, to express their own experience of the therapeutic work and this can be included within this section.

▶ Ending the workbook

As in all therapeutic approaches, consideration needs to be given to the way in which the work and the therapeutic relationship comes to an end. The structure of the workbook in terms of clearly labelled section numbers helps to highlight the stages of treatment to both the therapist and the patient. However, it is also useful to label this verbally with the young person at the beginning and end of each session, for example 'We're about halfway through the workbook now, and next week we're moving on to . . .' When therapists have a clear idea of the sessions remaining, it is particularly important to prepare the young person for this. We would encourage the therapist and young person to review progress before reaching the last section of the book in order to anticipate and arrange further help if necessary.

It is very important that the young person has their own copy of materials from the workbook to keep both in-between sessions and when they have completed the work. While working through *Hunger for Understanding*, the workbook can serve as transitional object and help the young person to hold on to the ideas discussed and utilise the benefits of the therapeutic relationship in-between sessions. Following therapy, the workbook materials can serve as an important reminder of the work completed.

Working with young people with anorexia nervosa is a tough task. There are several factors that make this process difficult: young people with anorexia nervosa often have not accepted there is a problem and, because of this, struggle to engage with treatment. The physical manifestation of the disorder in terms of low body weight can be extremely distressing and anxiety-provoking for professionals working with the young person. With no other psychiatric problem is there such a visual display of psychological distress. This distress can be exacerbated by anxious family members and in some instances anxious healthcare professionals. Furthermore, working in large multidisciplinary teams can be fraught with difficulties as everyone may have a slightly different approach to the young person.

The *Hunger for Understanding* workbook was devised with these factors in mind. As clinicians working in the field, we have experienced at first hand the anxieties that these problems create within a therapeutic setting. The workbook aims to provide an approach that is theoretically sound and practically manageable. We hope that it helps provide a structure, guidance and the much-needed injection of hope to clinicians who are desperately trying to help but feel overwhelmed by the enormity of their task.

Hunger for Understanding

The Workbook

Contents

Introduction to the workbook

Suffering from an eating disorder such as anorexia nervosa can be a very lonely, distressing and confusing experience. Most people sense that something needs to change in their life, that they cannot go on living with the restrictions that anorexia puts on their lives; but thinking about making a change and possibly breaking free from anorexia can also seem terrifying and, for some, unimaginable.

The *Hunger for Understanding* workbook is designed to help answer some of the questions you may have about anorexia. It may also help you to think about what getting better can involve and will hopefully give you some encouragement that it is possible.

It is important that you have someone you trust to help you through the workbook

The workbook presents different sections, including understanding more about anorexia, what can cause anorexia, what treatment and recovery may involve, myths and questions people often ask about anorexia and, finally, some inspiration from young people who have been where you are today, and have recovered.

In each section, there are some questions that may help you make sense of the information from your own experiences. It is very important that you have someone you trust to help you work through the workbook, as some of the information may raise very difficult feelings. Part of recovering from anorexia is being able to share these difficult feelings and work through them at your own pace. Having someone to talk through the information in this workbook is an excellent start.

What is anorexia nervosa?

This section will provide you with information about what anorexia nervosa is. Hopefully it will help you to understand more about the difficulties you may be experiencing, such as how anorexia affects your body, your emotions and your relationships with other people.

Believe it or not, anorexia has been recognised for over 100 years now and has affected many men and women of different ages, from all over the world. It is difficult to estimate how many people are affected by anorexia because eating disorders can make people feel very ashamed and feel quite alone. This means they often do not ask for help, and so don't receive any and suffer in silence. It is very important that you understand that you are not alone. More and more work is being done to understand how and why anorexia develops, so that we can treat it effectively.

The term 'anorexia' means loss of appetite and the term 'anorexia nervosa' means nervous loss of appetite. However, this is very misleading as most sufferers do not actually lose their appetite. Anorexia nervosa is a condition that drives people to want to lose weight. Most young people with anorexia are terrified of becoming fat and develop very strict eating routines, often avoiding particular foods. The most striking signs of anorexia are weight loss and a determination to avoid what others might consider a 'normal' intake of food. However, there may also be other signs such as:

► Fear of fatness – this is an intense fear of gaining weight or becoming fat.

▶ A belief that your body is larger than it is – you may feel fat even when you are very underweight. This is known as a distortion of body image and is part of the anorexia.

▶ A preoccupation with thoughts about food, eating, weight and/or calories – you may spend lots of time thinking about food, so much so that it interferes with other aspects of your life and affects your attention and concentration.

▶ Getting rid of food by purging – many young people with anorexia achieve weight loss through restricting their diet. However, up to 50 per cent may also make themselves sick or use laxatives after eating to 'prevent' the calories being absorbed by the body. These methods of weight control are NOT effective and can often result in serious damage to your health.

▶ Burning off calories using excessive exercise – this means engaging in very strict exercise routines, which may also interfere with other aspects of your life.

▶ Some people may also occasionally binge on large quantities of food that usually they would restrict themselves from eating, for example, crisps and chocolate. At these times they feel very out of control around food.

Anorexia affects people in very different ways and not everyone will have all of these symptoms.

▶ Who gets anorexia nervosa?

Lots of different types of people may experience anorexia, men and women, boys and girls, of all ages. Most estimates suggest that anorexia is more common in girls and women; however, young men and boys can suffer from it as well. It is found in all different ethnic groups and social classes.

Lots of different types of people, boy and girls, may experience anorexia

▶ Why does anorexia nervosa develop?

▶ Communicating feelings

There is more to anorexia than a desire to be thin. Anorexia is often thought to be a way of dealing with feelings that are difficult to communicate, such as anger, worry, guilt or sadness. Often it develops around times of change in a young person's life, such as starting at a new school, a change within the family or changes in your body such as puberty, or perhaps as a combination of all these factors.

These changes can sometimes cause young people to feel that their life is out of control. The feelings that come with these changes, such as sadness, anger, anxiety or guilt, may be difficult to communicate to family and friends in the usual ways. Young people with anorexia may feel that the only area of life that they can control is food intake and weight and through this they feel able to regain some control over their life. Unfortunately, in most cases, anorexia ends up controlling them.

 ## Coping with problems

For some young people anorexia can be a way of blocking out problems. The source of these problems could be related to many different areas of life, such as family issues, school pressures or other social pressures like friendships and special relationships. When young people feel out of control, dissatisfied or unhappy in these areas of their life, they may feel that focusing all their attention on food and weight temporarily helps to block out the things that are worrying them.

Self-esteem

Anorexia has also been linked to low self-esteem and self-confidence. This means that young people with anorexia often don't see themselves as important or worthwhile and will have a very negative view of themselves. For example, 'I'm a bad friend', 'No one likes me', 'I'm ugly'. These beliefs often hold the person back from taking risks and just 'having a go' at things that might help them feel better about themselves. Instead, what tends to happen is that they isolate themselves from others and this then 'proves' the belief that they are worthless and no good.

A person with anorexia may appear happy but inwardly be unhappy

When someone is in this trap of believing they are worthless, anorexia is one way that the person can begin to feel a sense of achievement as they have the control to starve their body of the food it needs. This sense of achievement doesn't last long, though. Soon the body is unable to keep up with the constant demands of anorexia and a sense of failure sets in.

While young people with anorexia may experience low self-esteem, they may also have very high expectations or set very high standards for themselves. Often they expect much more of themselves than they would expect of other people or their best friend, for example. Outwardly, they may well appear confident but usually inwardly they feel very unhappy.

In Section 2, 'What causes anorexia?', we will be looking at some other ideas about how anorexia develops.

Naming anorexia

Anorexia nervosa is the name that has been given to your difficulties. If you could rename your difficulties, so that it means something more to you, what name would you use and why?

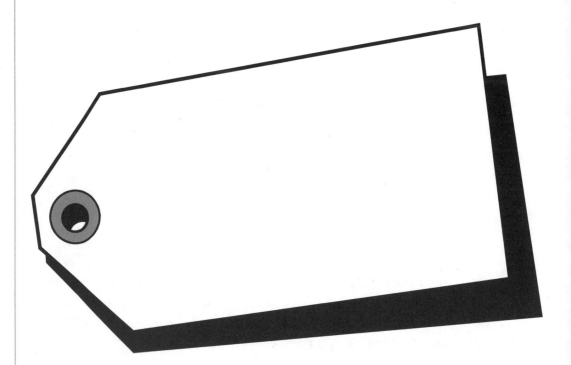

Similarities and differences

Although young people with anorexia share a lot in common, everyone's experience will be slightly different. This can be confusing and for some people this can allow them to go on pretending they don't have an eating disorder. Write a list of the things you feel you share in common with other people suffering from an eating disorder, and another list with the things that make your experience different.

Similarities

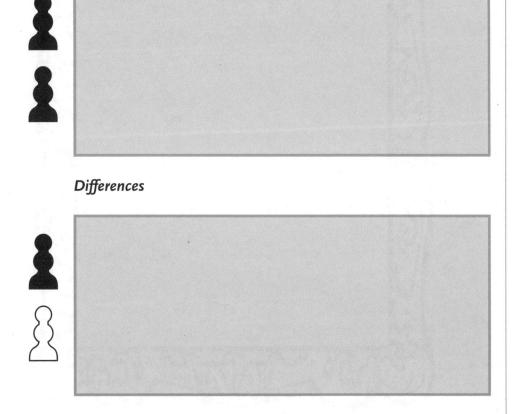

Differences

What does anorexia look like?

If you could see your anorexia, what do you think it would look like? Draw a picture of it in the space below. Think about the type of shape, size and colour it would be.

What causes anorexia?

Have you ever seen a television programme or read a book about anorexia? If so, you have probably heard or read about lots of different ideas and theories about what causes an eating disorder such as anorexia. If not, you are probably just as confused as those who have.

There are many, many different theories about the causes of anorexia, and lots of time has been devoted to research to find the exact 'cause' so that we can develop effective treatments. What the research has found is that there is no one single cause for anorexia. The reasons for one person developing anorexia can be very different from the next person's reasons.

In this section, we will be looking at the different factors that research has shown *may* lead on to anorexia, and we will then be thinking how these different theories relate to your own difficulties.

▶ A gradual development?

It is very rare that someone wakes up one morning to find that suddenly they have anorexia!! This may seem obvious, but sometimes people think that one single event or moment in time can cause anorexia. We now know that often anorexia is caused by more than one factor, and that different factors may combine over a period of time. It is sometimes helpful to look at these different factors over a person's lifetime to see how they might have combined to cause anorexia.

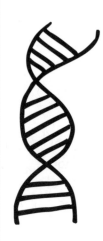

▶ Is it in our genes?

One theory is that our genes play an important part in the onset of anorexia. We inherit 'genes' from our biological parents. Each gene carries specific information and it is this information that determines certain characteristics about us, for example, what colour of eyes we have and what colour of hair we have.

Research has looked at the numbers of identical versus non-identical twins with anorexia and has found that when one twin has anorexia nervosa, the other is 10 times more likely to have it too, if they are identical. As identical twins have the same genes (this is what makes them 'identical'), this suggests that genes play an important role in the development of anorexia.

However, a major problem with genetic research into anorexia is trying to separate what is caused by genes and what is caused by the environment – this is everything around us that contributes to our experiences. It seems that genes may make someone more likely to develop an eating disorder, but there are often other events or experiences that happen to the individual that 'trigger' the onset.

▶ How does our environment affect the onset of anorexia?

We know that anorexia seems to occur in women more than men and mostly in women who live in developed countries where there is no shortage of food. It is probably no coincidence that, because there is no shortage of food, we live in a society that values slimness and frowns upon obesity.

As our society has become more focused on the possibilities of achieving a slim body (e.g. through various diets and exercise crazes), the numbers of people with eating disorders have increased. Also, in environments where there is greater pressure to achieve a slim body, such as dancing and gymnastics, there are higher rates of eating disorders such as anorexia.

Young men and women receive messages from the media (such as TV and magazines) about what their bodies should ideally look like. For boys there is a strong expectation that they should be physically fit, toned and muscular. Girls often feel that they are meant to have slim figures with non-existent thighs, hips and bottoms!

As their bodies change and develop around the time of puberty, young people can develop a sense of inadequacy or sometimes shame about their body which may not add up to what they regard as the ideal. In fact, there are many more men and women whose bodies do not fit the ideal image than those who do. Think about the figures of catwalk models and some TV and film stars – how many people do you know who match these standards?

However, only a few girls and boys go on to develop anorexia when nearly all have grown up with these unrealistic ideals, so 'cultural' explanations cannot fully explain the cause of anorexia.

How do families affect the onset of anorexia?

For some time now, researchers have attempted to see if there are things which families may have in common which may lead young people to develop anorexia. For example, there have been studies to look at the order in which brothers and sisters are born, the family size, the way that families communicate and how arguments and disagreements are sorted out.

In the 1970s, research suggested that young people with anorexia tended to come from families who were very involved with each other and avoided any conflict or arguments. However, there are many such families with children who have no problems or very different problems. There is some evidence, however, that having a parent who is forever on a diet, family disputes such as those relating to separation and divorce, illness within the family, and traumas such as abuse, can all make someone vulnerable to an eating disorder.

Although it seems that families are unlikely ever to be the sole cause of anorexia, research has suggested that the way that they respond to their child can make the situation better or worse. This is one of the reasons why family therapy is recommended for young people with anorexia. Although the family may not have been the cause of the anorexia, it can play a very important part in the recovery.

▶ What about personality?

You may already have noticed that you share some similarities with other young people with anorexia. Many research studies have looked into similarities in personality and life experiences among people with anorexia. For example, parents often describe their children who have developed the disorder as having been 'perfect children', who were well behaved, popular, hard-working and often achieved good results in school. However, this is not always the case, and many young people with anorexia nervosa do not have such tendencies.

A common factor in the development of anorexia is stress, perhaps caused by the demands of exams and schoolwork

Many young people who develop anorexia have struggled with feelings of sadness, anger, anxiety and guilt. They often have low self-esteem, see themselves as failures, bad or unworthy, and have a very negative view of the way they look.

Some researchers have argued that these personality characteristics can make young people vulnerable to stress. We know that anorexia nervosa normally starts in young people around the time of puberty, which is often a time of stress and change (such as physical changes in the body, as well as changes in terms of feelings, friendships and family relationships).

When a person feels overwhelmed or unprepared by the challenges of adolescence and puberty, they may feel that life is spiralling out of control. Their personality, as well as problems in communicating difficult feelings, may make it seem impossible to get through things on a day-to-day basis. There may also be other stresses on top of this, such as family arguments, an extra pressure to do well, the death of someone close, or a trauma (such as bullying, emotional, physical or sexual abuse).

Most young people with anorexia have, at some point, felt their life was out of control, and controlling food and eating may have been a way of coping or showing other people around them that they are not managing and need help.

As you can see, there is a whole range of different factors that can cause anorexia. Figure 2.1 may help to explain how together they can result in the development of an eating disorder.

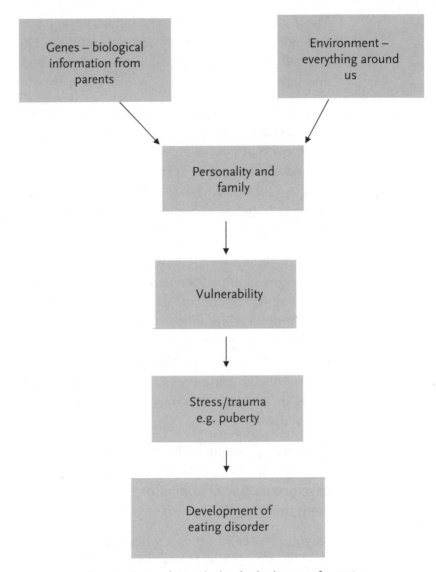

Figure 2.1 Factors that can lead to the development of anorexia

◀ TASK 2.1 ▶

Your story

Write your story about how your problem developed. Do not worry if there are gaps or you are unsure. Write down questions to come back to later.

_____
_____
_____
_____
_____
_____
_____
_____
_____
_____
_____
_____
_____
_____
_____
_____
_____
_____
_____
_____
_____
_____
_____
_____
_____
_____
_____

Life experiences

Think about the different experiences you've had in your life and how these have affected the way that you view your body.

Positive and negative influences

Which people have helped you to see yourself in a positive and a negative way?

Your journey

You may find it helpful to draw a timeline relating to your story. A timeline is where you think about certain things happening at certain times, in the order they occurred.

For example:

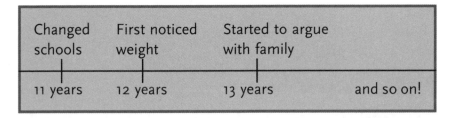

Changed schools	First noticed weight	Started to argue with family	
11 years	12 years	13 years	and so on!

Age/Date:

_____

Event:

◄ TASK 2.5 ►

Factors that may contribute to the development of anorexia

Can you think of anything you may have read in Section 2 that may have contributed to the development of anorexia for you?

 Things that have contributed to anorexia:

How does dieting affect us?

Eating disorders are caused by many different factors, but in almost all cases dieting is one of the main triggers for the onset of eating disorders such as anorexia nervosa. Often this may start out as quite harmless, but very soon it can start to dominate one's thinking, feelings and behaviour so that life feels as if it has become focused around food.

In this section, we will be looking more at the effects of dieting and how our bodies are designed to maintain a stable weight.

▶ What happens when we diet?

Our bodies are designed to keep weight around a set point. This means that we all have an individual range in which our weight will fluctuate, and this will vary from person to person depending on our genes. This is why our bodies put up such a battle when we attempt to lose weight.

For example, if Jenny's set-point weight is around 54 kg (8½ stones), her weight can vary comfortably within a range of, say, about 3 kg (half a stone, plus or minus) without her body noticing too much. If she attempts to lose about 6 kg (1 stone) in weight, her body will resist. It is a bit like compressing a spring. When the spring starts to get compressed, the body will resist by increasing the hunger drive and Jenny will feel as though she is thinking about food all the time. This is her body's attempt to return her weight to its normal range.

By ignoring her body's signals that she is hungry, Jenny will be replacing her body's automatic cues for hunger with conscious mental cues focusing on not eating. She will lose trust in her body's signals for hunger and, to prevent herself from lapsing from her diet, will be setting herself very strict rules about what she can and cannot eat. When the hunger gets the better of her, Jenny is likely to end up overeating (a bit like the spring bouncing back up again).

When a diet is broken, we usually end up eating more than we would have eaten before the diet. This is due to a mixture of the powerful hunger urges, the fact that we no longer trust our internal body cues and also thoughts along the lines of 'I've blown it, so I might as well eat everything'. This is why dieting often results in a higher set-point weight. It's a strange fact that yo-yo dieting makes us more likely to put on weight in the long term than if we allowed our weight to fluctuate within its normal range.

When a diet becomes so extreme that it turns into starvation, our bodies fight back by slowing down the metabolic rate and storing as much food as possible. This makes it much harder to lose weight on even very few calories. Soon the emotional effects of weight loss such as poor concentration and irritability add to the person's sense of feeling more out of control of their eating and even more of a failure.

▶ How does dieting affect the way we feel?

In the 1950s, a research study (Keys et al., 1950) found some fascinating results that help us to understand the effects of dieting and starvation in eating disorders today. A researcher called Ancel Keys asked 36 healthy men to participate in his study. The men were monitored closely during the first three months while their eating patterns and personalities were studied. They were then put on a strict diet and their normal food intake was halved for three months. In the final part of the study the men were reintroduced to eating normal amounts of food.

The researchers' observations astounded them. Food became the main topic of conversation for all the men during the three-month starvation period. Many of the men began dreaming about food, and were fascinated by cookery books and menus. Some of the men found it impossible to stick to the diet and secretly ate on impulse, and expressed feeling extremely guilty after doing so. Emotionally, the men became more anxious and depressed and had trouble concentrating. They also began to withdraw from other people and were much less sociable and friendly. Some of the men who had no previous concerns about their body image became more critical of their bodies, and some complained of being overweight, even though they had *lost* weight.

When they were introduced to normal eating again, many of them felt as though they would not be able to stop eating when they were full, and found it difficult to estimate what was a normal portion of food. Their normal eating habits returned after a period of time of eating normally and they also lost their intense focus on food.

So reducing food intake over an extended period of time seems to have very powerful effects, not only on our bodies, but also the way we think and feel. The experiences of these men back in 1950 are not dissimilar to the thoughts, feelings and behaviours reported by many women and men struggling with an eating disorder today.

It seems that some of the symptoms of eating disorders (such as thinking about food a lot of the time) are a direct result of our bodies being starved or considerably below our normal 'set point'. This is important to know as, all too often, individuals who are suffering with eating disorders believe that their thoughts about food prove that they are a weak person whose hunger needs to be controlled. In fact, most people would experience the same feelings of anxiety and depression, preoccupation with food and negative thoughts about their body and shape when their bodies are being starved, it is simply the normal human response to starvation.

Most people would feel anxious, depressed and preoccupied about food if they were not eating properly

The Keys experiment helps us to understand how important it is to get back to a healthy weight range. Although it is extremely scary for someone suffering with anorexia to even think about putting on 1kg (a few pounds), it has been found that many of the powerful effects of starvation are resolved when the normal weight range is reached. Of course, there are other important parts to the treatment, but eating regular meals and gradually getting back to a healthy weight range is an essential part of recovering from anorexia. We will be thinking about this more in Section 8, 'Getting better'.

◀ TASK 3.1 ▶

Anorexia's choice

If anorexia could choose what you had to eat and drink in a day, what would it look like? Draw it on the plates below, thinking about breakfast, lunch, evening meal and any snacks.

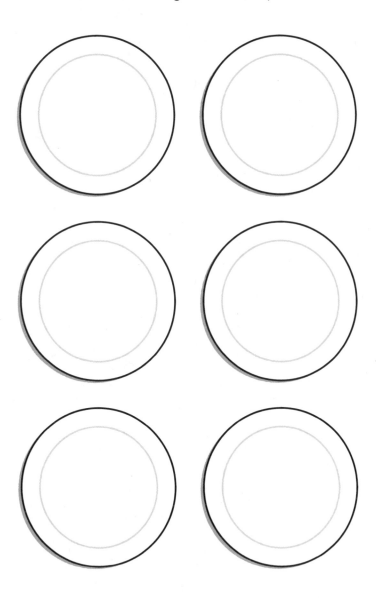

A typical meal before anorexia

On the plates below, draw what you used to eat and drink in a typical day before you had anorexia.

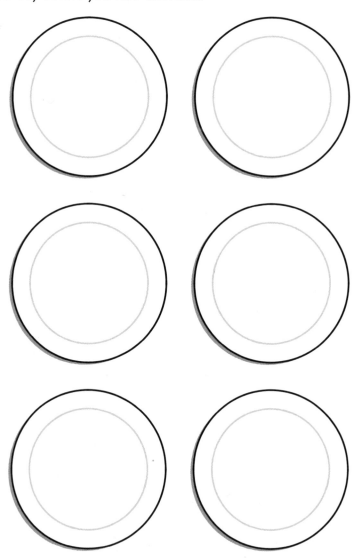

A healthy choice

On the final set of plates, draw what you think a healthy day of food and drink would look like. This would mean that you have enough calories to maintain your weight in a healthy range.

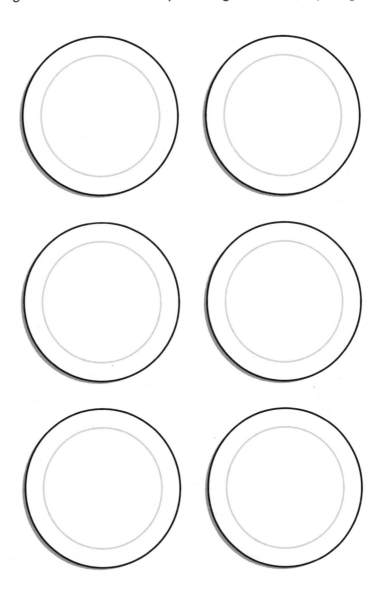

◄ TASK 3.4 ►

Compare the plates!

What differences and similarities do you notice about the meals you have drawn?

Similarities

Differences

Good and bad food

Anorexia has a way of dividing food into good and bad choices, rather than allowing us to see that we need a whole range of foods to give us the nutrition our bodies need. What foods does anorexia tell you are bad/forbidden and what foods does it tell you are good/safer?

Good food   *Bad food*

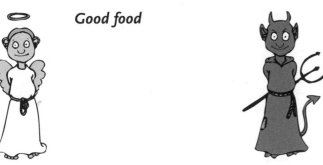

Do YOU agree?

How does anorexia affect you?

As you may be aware, anorexia affects us in more ways than just our body size. In this section, we will be looking more at the ways anorexia can affect us as a whole, including how we think, how we feel, our relationships and the way we behave. We will also be looking at some facts about the short- and long-term damage anorexia can do.

▶ Changes in the way you think and see things

Anorexia can affect the way that you think about things. You may find yourself thinking about food a lot of the time, to the extent that it interferes with your normal life.

Many young people with anorexia experience disturbances in the way they see things. These disturbances in perception are part of the illness and may make you think you are bigger and fatter than you really are. Even though your body is underweight, you see yourself as bigger than other people see you. You may think that certain parts of your body are bigger, particularly your stomach, bottom or thighs. These disturbances feel very real and can cause a lot of distress, even though your body is underweight.

▶ Changes in the way you feel

Many young people with anorexia experience an intense fear of gaining weight and in many cases this can lead to feeling very low in mood and very anxious about getting better. You may feel you are failing to meet the goals you have set yourself and feel very powerless. This may make you feel very uncertain about being able to recover and put anorexia behind you. These types of feelings can often lead to you becoming very withdrawn and feeling locked into a very lonely world where you feel you can keep yourself safe by not eating.

Anorexia can make you feel very lonely

▶ Changes in what you do

You may have stopped doing the things you normally do, such as going out with friends, taking part in hobbies or doing things you used to enjoy. It can feel as though thinking about food is taking up most of your time.

You are likely to be restricting what you eat or eating as little as possible. However, you may also occasionally:

▶ Binge – eat lots of food in short bursts.

▶ Vomit – make yourself sick after you have eaten.

▶ Use diet pills or laxatives.

▶ Do lots of exercise.

In many instances, these behaviours develop as a means of trying to make up for foods you have eaten.

In some cases, schoolwork may have become difficult. You may be trying very hard to keep up with your work, but have trouble concentrating. You may also be very hard on yourself when you make mistakes or have lost confidence in your abilities.

▶ Effects on your body

Anorexia can affect the body in many different ways, depending on factors such as how long you have suffered from anorexia. The information in this section can be quite alarming. Although it is not intended to shock you, it is important that you are aware of the serious damage anorexia can do to your body. Fortunately, nearly all of the symptoms can be reversed, but only when you return to a healthy weight and, if you are female, when your periods return. Unfortunately, a small number of people die from anorexia each year, due to the extreme effects it has on the body.

▶ *Extreme tiredness and feeling weak.* When food intake is reduced, your body turns to the fat reserves it has to feed itself. If there is little or no fat left to lose, it will turn to muscle as a source of energy. In very extreme cases, this includes the heart muscle; you are literally digesting yourself. Because your muscles are not getting the nutrients they need, you may find some physical activities very difficult, such as climbing the stairs, standing up from squatting, and you may also notice that you are clumsier. All these are signs that your body is struggling to keep going.

Energy levels vary a lot, depending on the stage of anorexia. Some people find they have more energy in the early stages. This is the body's attempt to get you to find and eat food. Other people say they feel tired all the time, and, again, this is the body's way of saving energy and body tissue.

▶ *Feeling shivery, cold and dizzy.* These symptoms are due to starvation and loss of body fat, which we need to insulate us from the cold. Also blood pressure drops because the heart muscle is weaker. This makes it more difficult for the heart to pump blood around the body, which can cause chest pains, heart flutterings, dizziness and fainting.

▶ *Constipation, diarrhoea and bladder problems.* The system that deals with the digestion of food (gastro-intestinal system) shrinks if the body is continually starved. This can make you feel full even after only a small amount of food or drink. Starvation also makes it difficult for the body to digest food and so bacteria will grow faster in the small bowel. This can cause constipation and this is extremely uncomfortable and painful. The bladder and bowel muscles are weakened and this can cause incontinence problems such as wetting and soiling.

▶ *Impact on fertility (ability to have children).* In young women, starvation can cause the ovaries and uterus to shrink. This may mean that periods become infrequent or stop (something known as amenorrhoea). In young men, sperm production may be affected. Both these things can have an impact on fertility and in some instances it may be harder to have children.

▶ *Swollen ankles, swollen hands, cold hands and feet.* These symptoms are all due to poor circulation.

▶ *Symptoms you can't see.* Anorexia can cause your bones to thin and become brittle (osteoporosis), muscle wastage, brain shrinkage, kidney damage, damage to your immune system (ability to fight off illnesses), weakening of the heart muscle and low white blood cells (the cells that fight infection).

▶ *Cuts* do not heal as well.

▶ *Vomiting food* can cause tooth decay which is very difficult to repair and can leave you with lasting pain.

▶ *Effects on the way you look.* People with anorexia often look much older than they really are. This is because of the loss of muscle. Their skin is usually dry, pale and can sometimes have a green or yellow tinge to it. The hair is also often dry and in some cases hair can fall out. Some people grow more body hair. Lips can be broken or cracked and the palms can appear orange.

▶ *Taking laxatives* can alter your blood chemistry so that you may have higher levels of potassium in the blood. This is extremely dangerous and can increase the risk of sudden collapse.

If you are worried about any of these things, it is always a good idea to talk over your worries with someone else.

▶ Effects on other people around you

Young people with anorexia may find it hard to keep up with pressures at school because of problems concentrating and the energy that is taken up by anorexia. Teachers and friends may have noticed you becoming more withdrawn and not seeming your normal self.

The illness has a huge effect on family relationships. Mealtimes can become very stressful for everyone involved as your parents will often feel it is their duty to help you get back to a healthy weight. Sometimes they may react in ways that you don't find helpful, such as becoming extremely angry with you.

Because anorexia has a way of fooling people into thinking they are really 'OK', you may find it hard to understand your parents' or friends' concern. Their angry reactions are most likely to be their frustration at what anorexia is doing to you. Parents and friends will be able to help you if they can understand the battles you are having with anorexia. If you can try to explain these to them and let them know how to help you, they can battle with you on your side, so that you do not feel so alone. This can be hard, but it is worth a try.

Anorexia's body image

We've heard about how anorexia can make you feel as though your body is bigger than it really is. In the space below, draw a picture or an outline of how you think your body looks at the moment. You might also draw some of the ways your anorexia has affected your body and the way you look.

Other people's image

In the space below, draw a picture of how you think other people (like your best friend, or mum or dad) might see your body. If this is difficult for you, ask someone you trust to have a go.

Comparing images

What differences do you notice between the two bodies you have drawn?

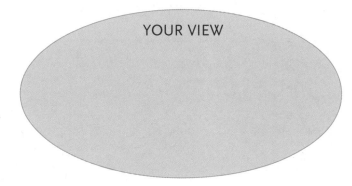

YOUR VIEW

OTHERS' VIEW

◄ TASK 4.4 ►

The losses from having anorexia

What has anorexia taken away from you? Think about your relationships, activities, interests and skills. What other ways has it affected you and your family?

What keeps anorexia going?

Once anorexia has developed, there are lots of different factors that keep it going and make change seem difficult. What keeps anorexia going can sometimes be very different to what triggered the problem in the first place. Therefore, it is important to understand the factors that may keep anorexia in your life, so that you can work on them directly.

The physical effects of starvation mean that you may have become used to having very little food. It may be difficult to know when you are feeling hungry and when you need to be eating. Losing weight will have made you feel in control, and this in itself can be very rewarding. This can make weight gain very difficult and quite frightening in the beginning. Body image distortion (when you see yourself as much bigger than you actually are), along with lots of negative thoughts about food and eating, will also make it harder to begin eating again.

Feeling quite down and anxious may also make you feel that you really can't get better. You may not have the confidence to try to change some of your behaviours. These feelings are related to the anorexia and keep it going.

People around you such as your parents, your brothers and/or sisters may not fully understand anorexia and, because of this, they may do certain things that also maintain it. Anorexia has a way of making you feel alone and separating you from your family and friends so that you feel unable to trust them. That is why it is very important that the people closest to you understand what anorexia is and how it affects you.

Anorexia has a way of making you feel alone and separating you from friends and family

Other factors outside you and your family may also help maintain anorexia, such as pressure from other sources, friends at school, magazines and other media to stay thin may make it hard for you to take up normal healthy eating again.

As you can see, there are lots of factors that will be working to maintain anorexia. An awareness of these will help you to understand more about how to overcome some of these difficulties. We will be thinking more about this in Section 8, 'Getting better'.

What keeps anorexia going for you?

  ▶

 ▶

▶

 ▶

What do you value about it?

What would you be scared to lose?

Closeness circles

Place the people you know (friends and family) in the sections of the circle in terms of how close you feel to them right now. For example, you might want to place a friend whom you can really trust and talk to in the middle of the circle.

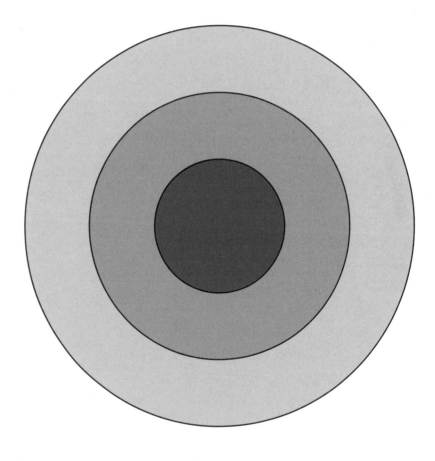

Key:

■	■	■
Very close to me	Close to me	Not close to me

In my ideal world

Then, in a different colour pen, place people where you would *ideally* like them to be. There may be some people who need to be further away from you and others whom you would love to be closer.

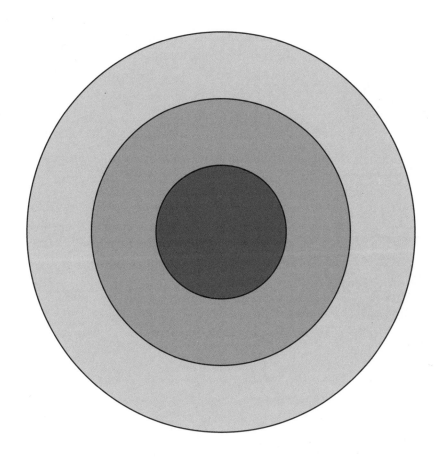

Key:

█ Very close to me   █ Close to me   █ Not close to me

How anorexia affects closeness

Take a good look at where you have placed people and notice where there are differences in where people are and where you would like them to be.

Has anorexia affected how close you feel to people?

What might the circles look like when anorexia is not in your life?

The tricks anorexia plays

Anorexia is extremely clever. If it took exams in deception, it would come top of the class every time! It can fool the most intelligent people and make them believe that everything it tells them is true.

In this section, we will be looking at some of the clever tricks that anorexia can play. It is very important that you are aware of them, because in order to be able to battle against anorexia, you need to know what is 'real' and what games anorexia is playing with you.

▶ 'I'm your best friend'

As we're now aware, anorexia tends to strike people when they feel very low. You may feel out of control and as though no one understands you. That's when anorexia can sneak into your life and cleverly convince you that it is there to solve all your problems and make you feel better. To begin with, anorexia can seem like your best friend. It can be very reassuring and tells you that things will be OK if you lose weight and control the amount you eat. It sets you targets and gives you a huge pat on the back when you manage to reach them.

To begin with, anorexia can seem like your best friend

Anorexia also gives you something to focus on and take your mind off other worries. Many people say that to begin with, anorexia helped them to cope with some tough times. Not surprisingly, it can convince you that losing weight is the solution to all your problems, and that putting on weight will be disastrous. When life is in turmoil, anorexia can at times feel like a very good friend.

'The worst bully'

Soon, though, anorexia can turn from being friendly and supportive to being harsh, critical and bullying. It's never satisfied with your efforts and even when you have achieved its targets, it sets you harder and more impossible tasks to achieve.

Anorexia sometimes tells you to punish yourself for things you have done which it doesn't agree with. For example, because you had some lunch, you have to exercise for a certain amount of time. You may end up doing some very strange things that look weird to other people, but make sense to you and to anorexia.

Anorexia can turn into a bully, being harsh and critical

Sometimes the voice of anorexia changes from being reassuring and positive to being angry and abusive. It can feel like constant harassment in your ear that is unbearable. It tells you to lie to people and makes you feel more and more distant from those around you. It tells you not to trust or show feelings to anyone else but itself. Anorexia cleverly makes you feel that you are worthless and nothing without it and makes it almost impossible to think about life at a normal weight.

How clever is your anorexia?

What tricks have you noticed anorexia playing on you?

▶ Trick 1

▶ Trick 2

▶ Trick 3

◀ TASK 6.2 ▶

My best friend

Think about the times when anorexia has seemed like your best friend. How did it convince you of this?

The bully

When has anorexia been a horrible bully?

The future

What messages does anorexia give you about your future, with and without it in your life?

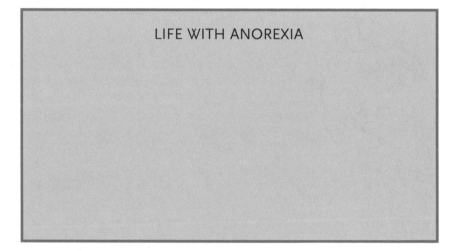

LIFE WITH ANOREXIA

LIFE WITHOUT ANOREXIA

Thinking about change

As we have already seen, there is a mixture of positive and negative symptoms with anorexia, such as a sense of achievement but also feeling depressed and anxious. People often ask the question 'Why can't you just eat?' as if eating will make the problem go away. We know that it takes a combination of two approaches to recover from anorexia:

1 To understand how anorexia has become a means of coping and then to develop other ways of dealing with difficult feelings and situations.

2 To get weight back within a normal range to prevent the long-term physical effects of anorexia.

This may sound very simple, but both issues are hard to face, and take time and hard work. Often thinking about getting better can bring a mixture of relief, 'Thank goodness I don't have to pretend everything's OK any more', but also a huge amount of fear, 'I'll have to eat now'. It is *very* normal to have mixed feelings about getting better.

> **“**It's like you're two people; one who wants to get rid of the eating disorder and one who doesn't. Even the thought of putting on weight makes you feel sick. I couldn't imagine how I would cope without my protection, my form of identity, my friend, my enemy. What if I couldn't stop eating and end up really fat?**”**
>
> *Katie, 16 years old*

Often life has become completely organised around food, weight and calories, and although anorexia can be very punishing at times, it may also give you a false sense of safety and control. At first, you probably felt as though you were in control, but there comes a point where anorexia has taken over your life, as this person discovered:

> *I knew when I needed professional help. My head was in such a state of confusion and I had no understanding of what was happening to me. I was being controlled by something that could not be seen, heard or even touched, just felt very much emotionally. I was not me any more. I was just a person being controlled by something not even visible. I wanted to know more about what was happening to me, why I felt this way, why I had no control over my own thoughts.*
>
> ### Amy, 17 years old

Treatment is about getting back real control over your body, your thoughts, beliefs and your life. It is about gradually breaking free from the strict patterns of control that anorexia has placed on you and your life.

> *Looking back, I realised that it feels much worse to begin with as you have to cope with your problems and not hide behind the eating disorder.*
>
> ### James, 15 years old

You are probably now aware that anorexia will never let go of its own accord; it won't let you ever have the perfect body, or be thin enough. It will always add new rules that drive you further and further away from your friends, your family and, most importantly, yourself.

"An eating disorder is not something that you can go on with and expect to ever have a normal happy life. The only way to recover is to admit to yourself that you need help and be willing to give others the right to help you fight for your life."

Charlotte, 13 years old

"Getting better is not about getting rid of your fears. It's about moving forward in spite of them."

Jessica, 18 years old

An important message to keep in mind is that when you start treatment, you are not giving up control but you will be taking charge again. Without help and treatment, you are not in control – anorexia is. If you have worked through this workbook so far, you may already be starting to understand why anorexia became a solution to some of the difficulties you have been experiencing.

It is important for you to remember that you did not catch anorexia like a cold! Likewise, it does not mean that you are crazy or attention-seeking. You probably developed anorexia because it was a solution to some of your problems or helped you cope with very difficult feelings. Sometimes looking at the good parts of anorexia can help you understand why it is hard to consider giving it up.

How anorexia helps

In the space below, make a list of all the advantages or helpful aspects of having anorexia.

_____

_____

_____

_____

_____

_____

_____

_____

_____

_____

_____

_____

_____

_____

_____

_____

_____

_____

Do not worry if there are more advantages than disadvantages, just think about how anorexia became a solution for you. Think about some of the positives/advantages you have put down and take some time to look at them with a friend or someone you

How anorexia hinders

Now think about some of the problems with anorexia, e.g. how it stops you from doing the things you want to do.

_____
_____
_____
_____
_____
_____
_____
_____
_____
_____
_____
_____
_____
_____
_____
_____
_____
_____

trust, or the person who is doing this workbook with you. Ask yourself if this really is positive or think about what it would be like in the future if you still had anorexia. For example, what would you miss out on? It is a good idea to do this piece of work with a person who is not also suffering from anorexia.

Farewell letter

Sometimes thinking about saying goodbye to anorexia can seem like saying goodbye to a good friend. You may feel extremely sad about this, and one way to deal with these feelings of sadness and loss is to write a letter to your anorexia as though you are saying goodbye. Write about all the good times you have had, what you will miss not having it around, and how you will cope without it.

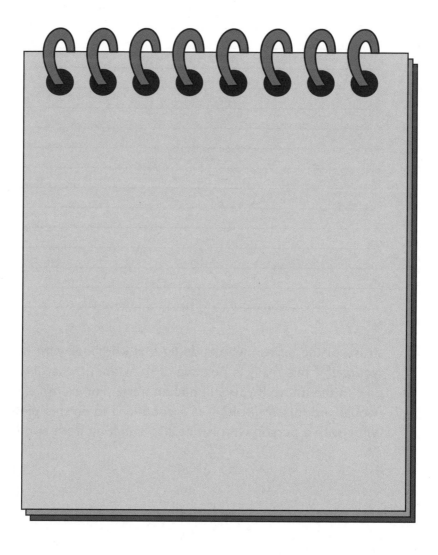

Stages of readiness to change

The professionals who will be helping you overcome anorexia will need to know how you feel about starting to change your eating. This is important so that they can work at a pace that is suitable for you. When people think about working on a problem, they usually go through six stages of 'readiness' to change. These are:

Stage 1   You may not have thought about the possibility of change, and probably did not ask for help.

Stage 2   You are thinking about change, but are probably not convinced that you need help or you're unsure or frightened about giving up anorexia.

Stage 3   You know you want to change and overcome anorexia.

Stage 4   You start to make some steps towards changing.

Stage 5   The changes are becoming easier and you might be thinking of a future without anorexia.

Stage 6   You temporarily go back to using food as a way of coping.

Success!   Usually after going through these stages a few times, you find ways of managing to overcome anorexia.

Normally, people don't tend to move straight from Stage 1 through to success. Usually, people find that they go up and down the stages. So, for example, you may find that one day you feel very much in Stage 1, not wanting to change, and the next day something happens which makes you determined to change and you feel as though you are in Stage 3.

It is normal to feel uncertain about change, and as the stages suggest, it can mean going from good to bad days many times before you manage to achieve control over anorexia. Moving from a good to a bad day does not mean you have failed. Whether you are aware of it or not, you and the team working with you will have learnt something that will help you move on again when you are ready.

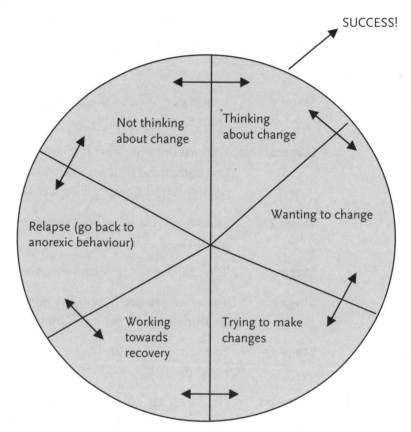

Figure 7.1 The cycle of change
Source: Adapted from Prochaska and DiClemente (1992)

Importance of change

Using the scale below (0 = not important and 10 = extremely important), rate how important it is for you to overcome anorexia. Put the date by the number and come back to this another time to see how it changes.

10 Extremely important

9
8

7

6

5

4

3

2

1

0 Not important

Reasons for change

Write a list of the reasons why you feel it is important to overcome anorexia, now and in the future.

Where are you?

Looking at the six stages of readiness to change, where do you think you are? Where have you come from and where do you want to get to?

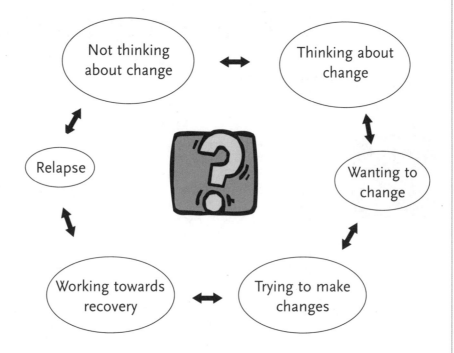

What would need to happen to move your readiness to change up one stage?

◄ TASK 7.7 ►

Level of confidence

Using this scale (0 = no confidence and 10 = extremely confident), rate how confident you feel that you will be able to overcome anorexia. Put the date by the number and come back to this another time to see how it changes.

10 Extremely confident

9
8

7

6

5

4

3
2

1

0 Not confident

Challenges I've faced before

Think about times in your life when you had to overcome an obstacle in your life. What were they? How did you manage to overcome them? What qualities do you have that helped you to succeed? How might these qualities help you to overcome anorexia?

OBSTACLES

OVERCOMING OBSTACLES

QUALITIES FOR SUCCESS

OVERCOMING ANOREXIA

Getting better

How can you be cleverer than anorexia? It is possible, but it takes a lot of effort and the support of those around you. In this section, we will be looking at what *you* can do to overcome anorexia. Much of this advice has come from people who have recovered from anorexia.

'Anorexia defeated': with a lot of effort and support, you can overcome anorexia

1 Recognising anorexia

The first step is recognising that anorexia has sneaked into your life. This can be more difficult than it sounds, particularly if it has been good at convincing you that it is your best friend. It will make you feel as though you are a traitor by going against it and you may feel extremely guilty. These are all normal feelings to have at this stage, although you will need support to talk them through with someone.

Log it!

Keep a diary of when you notice anorexia pops into your mind. It may also be helpful to log any times of the day when you managed to shut anorexia out and what was happening at this time.

2 Recognising our 'rules for living'

We all have rules or beliefs that we carry in our heads to help us make sense of what happens to us. Some rules can be really helpful, for example, 'I may not be perfect but I can try my best' or 'It's OK to make mistakes, I can learn from them'. Other rules can be very fixed and very negative, such as, 'I must be thin for people to like me' or 'I must never get angry'.

We might not always be aware of these rules, but they can affect what we do and how we feel. So, for example, if one of my rules for living is, 'I must be thin to feel in control', I may only feel OK about myself when I can fit into a certain pair of jeans and feel depressed, anxious and upset if they ever feel tight. When I feel I have broken this rule, I may punish myself by exercising or not eating. This often confirms to us how much we need the rule and we end up placing even stricter rules upon ourselves to stop us from feeling out of control.

◀ TASK 8.2 ▶

Rules for living that you have in your life

What are the different rules for living that you are aware of?

Which ones do you think are healthy and helpful rules and which ones make you feel bad about yourself?

Helpful rules

_____
_____
_____
_____
_____
_____

Bad rules

_____
_____
_____
_____
_____
_____

▇3 Trusting others

The next step is to allow yourself to trust the people who are trying to help you. Anorexia is very powerful and it is extremely difficult to overcome it alone. The professional people around you are there to show how anorexia crept into your life and they understand the battle you are having. If you allow them to understand, they can work with you, at your pace, to help find ways of battling against it. Families also have a very important part to play in your recovery. Without knowing it, they can sometimes say and do things that are unhelpful. You and the professionals can guide them and help them to understand so that they become part of your team.

How others can help or hinder

Who are the people that can help you overcome anorexia?

What things can they do that can support you?

What unhelpful things might they do?

How could you let them know what you need from them?

■4 Test out the lies

Anorexia will have told you lots and lots of lies. Like, for example, that you will put on such an enormous amount of weight if you don't exercise for so many hours each day. In order to break free from these lies and deception, you will need to test some of them out for yourself. This will be a difficult time, but you will have the support of the team around you. The best way of proving anorexia is wrong is to set yourself a test to find out. So, for example, don't do what it tells you to for a period of time – allow yourself an anorexia-free hour, morning, day or whatever you feel able to do. When you have tried this test, ask yourself if your worst fears really came true.

◀ TASK 8.4 ▶

My anorexia-free time

Make a record of what happened during your anorexia-free time, for example, what you did instead, how you were feeling, what you thought about.

What you did

What you felt

What you thought

5 Fish for the healthy thoughts

If anorexia has been around for a while, your own healthy thoughts and anorexic thoughts will have got tangled up. The next step is to try to work out which ones need paying attention to and which ones you let go of. It's a bit like a fishing net; you only want the positive, helpful, healthy thoughts to get caught in the net, and allow the negative, critical anorexic thoughts to drop through the net. This can be very difficult and takes a lot of working at.

Sometimes you find a particular thought hanging around in your head that just won't drop through the net. If this happens, it sometimes helps to write it down on paper to get it out of your head and take a good look at it. If you know it's rubbish, an unhelpful thought that has no truth, then rip it up, flush it down the loo or burn it! If you're uncertain whether to believe it or not, go and check it out with someone you trust, or write down as many alternative ideas as you can think of.

Fishing for thoughts

So, for example, one negative, unhelpful thought might be 'People are looking at me and are thinking I'm greedy because I've eaten so much'. In the bubbles below, write out as many positive helpful thoughts as you can that challenge this idea.

What would my best friend say?

If you have trouble letting go of a horrible thought or image of yourself, ask 'What would my best friend (or someone that knows you really well) say if they knew I felt this way about myself?' Put yourself in their shoes for a minute and write down what you imagine they might say.

Be your own agony aunt

If a friend came to you with the problems you are facing, what good advice would you give her?

Dear friend,

Yours,

▊6 Remember what you're working for

Remind yourself that recovery is not about *giving up* control, it's about *you taking charge*. In the next task, write down all the different things you will be able to do when anorexia no longer has control of you.

You can do other things once anorexia is no longer in control

When anorexia is no longer in control, I will . . .

7 Find ways of looking after yourself

Anorexia is cruel and punishing and it is vital that you fight against this by actively doing things that are good for you. It is virtually impossible to be cruel and kind to ourselves at the same time! So if you can find things to do to look after yourself, you will not only be allowing less time for anorexia to punish you, but you will also be proving to yourself that you are worthwhile.

There are lots of ways to take care of yourself, like listening to your favourite band or singer, playing games with your mates, or watching favourite programmes and films with your friends.

Taking care of myself

In the space below, write down as many ways of looking after yourself as you can think of.

8 Keep a diary or journal

Often the thoughts in our heads can get very jumbled up and make us feel very confused. It can help to keep a diary of these different thoughts and feelings, as well as the events that caused them. A diary can be like a friend who you can tell absolutely anything to but you don't have to worry about their reaction. It can help to look back at things that have happened and see how you dealt with it. You can learn from what you did and think about what you might do differently in the future.

You could also go back over your entries and highlight passages or events that you want to hold on to. In a different colour, you could highlight the things you now see differently, for example, the anorexic thoughts and what they made you do. Sometimes it's also helpful when preparing yourself for things which you may want to talk about with someone, by allowing yourself time to think about them first.

9 Take one day at a time

None of us learned to ride a bike first go, and no one would expect you to overcome your eating difficulties all at once. It can feel like a bit of a rollercoaster ride and you may have really good days when you're able to put anorexia aside and other days when you feel really tortured by it again. It takes time, effort, practice and support to overcome anorexia and we can all learn from our mistakes.

A reminder to myself

If you've had a bad day, talk with someone or write about it in your diary. Remind yourself of things you have achieved so far and the reasons you want to keep on working at it.

▮10 Practice makes perfect

Remember that it will be some time before eating normally comes naturally. It *will* feel very false, unusual and uncomfortable to begin with. This is because of the changes that have happened to your body and the thoughts which anorexia has made you believe. To overcome the eating problems, you will need to force yourself to battle against the anorexic voice. It will require *you* to make choices which anorexia will want to punish you for. Remember that the choices you are being asked to make are directing you towards a life free from anorexic control. It will be some time before these healthy choices become more natural and regular practice will make it much easier.

▌11 Distract yourself

At times anorexic thoughts can become extremely loud in your head and can be very overwhelming. It is helpful to have some emergency techniques to help gain some control over them at such times. Distraction techniques help our brains to refocus on something else. Below are a few examples to practise.

▶ *Parcel up the thought or image*
Imagine wrapping up the thought (or image) in packaging that keeps it secure. It may be that it needs a very strong container to do this, like a trunk with a big lock on it. Imagine placing the package somewhere that feels right for you. It may be that you need to put it a long way away, like imagine it dropping to the bottom of the ocean, or you feel happier to let it float like a balloon on the end of a string and pay attention to it later on in the day.

▶ *The breathing triangle*
Sometimes anorexic thoughts can make you feel quite panicky and out of breath. The triangle can help you take control of breathing while also taking your mind off the distressing thought. Using the triangle below, focus your eyes at the bottom and breathe in slowly through your nose for one second and at the same time move your eyes to the top left corner. Hold your breath in for one second as you move your eyes from the top left corner to the top right corner. Then breathe out through your mouth as your eyes travel back down towards the bottom of the triangle. Repeat this 10 times or until you feel your breathing has calmed down and you feel more in control of the thoughts or images in your mind.

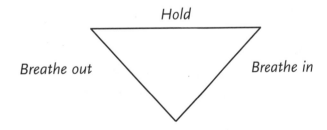

▶ *Exercises for the brain!*
Any mental activity that uses energy and effort can help take your mind away from anorexia. Here are a few ideas:

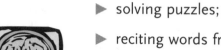

- ▶ solving puzzles;

- ▶ reciting words from songs;

- ▶ counting backwards from 100 in threes;

- ▶ going through the months of the year in reverse order;

- ▶ imagining what you would do if you won one million pounds!;

- ▶ making up an imaginary story about the people and things you can see.

▶ *Listen to music*
Most people have a song or piece of music that brings back happy memories, of a holiday, for example. Have this piece of music somewhere easy to reach at times when you are struggling. It may help to carry a Walkman around so that you can control the volume.

▶ *A survival message to yourself*
Write yourself a message that will help you at really difficult times. It may be a poem, words from a song or a reminder of a good piece of advice. Keep it in your pocket or rehearse it off by heart so you can remind yourself of it when you need to.

▶ *Carry your own symbol or object*
This might be a photograph, a stone/pebble or something that you enjoy the feel of, like a soft feather.

12 Remind yourself why NOT to give into anorexia

The list below gives some reasons why not to give into anorexia and may be helpful to remind yourself of when you need to.

▶ The problem isn't food, calories and weight, it's about your feelings. Giving into anorexia may put the problems in a deep freeze but *will not* help you to solve them.

▶ Anorexia will never be satisfied, no matter what you weigh.

▶ The more you give into the anorexic voice, the weaker you become to do battle!

▶ Anorexia makes you judge the success of your day on how much you've eaten, how you've managed to deceive others, the number on the weighing scales. Is this the way you really want to judge the success of your day?

How can I help myself?

Thinking about breaking free from anorexia is a bit like going on an uncertain journey. There are likely to be some difficult times ahead, as well as some wonderful discoveries. What things would you want to take with you on this journey to help you cope with the good and the bad times? You may want to think about taking special memories, past achievements, messages from people and maybe some of the things you have learned from working through this book.

Draw a suitcase or rucksack to hold all these important things in, and think about where you want to place them in the suitcase and how much room you want to give them.

Teamwork

There are lots of ways that we can work together to help you overcome anorexia. One important aspect in all of this is the idea of everyone pulling in the same direction. This means that everyone involved in helping you, healthcare professionals, teachers, family and friends, trusts each other to work closely together.

An important step in helping you to overcome anorexia is helping you and your family to understand more about it. This workbook is aimed at helping you understand more, but there are also other sources of information and education available to you.

In this section, we will be looking in more detail about the kinds of help you may need to recover from anorexia, and what the different parts of the treatment will involve.

 ## Getting back to the set-point range

One of the first tasks of overcoming anorexia is to gradually work towards a healthy weight range. This will mean increasing the amount of food you eat while not over-exercising, vomiting, taking laxatives, etc., as a way of compensating for the extra calories eaten. This is likely to be very difficult to begin with and you will need support to help you with the difficult thoughts and feelings you will probably be having at this time.

There are a number of different people who can help you get back to a healthy weight range and support you with the feelings you are having. Your family will play an important role in monitoring what you eat and helping you with any urges you may have to exercise, for example. Teachers or school nurses may also be sympathetic people to talk to when you need someone to discuss your fears with. You may also need the professional help of people like dieticians, psychiatrists, psychologists, nurses or occupational therapists. These people are trained to help young people overcome problems and will be able to offer advice while also giving you the opportunity to talk about your feelings.

You will need advice on the foods you require to steadily gain weight. If you have not been eating properly for a long time, you may be advised to eat quite small portions of food at first that will then build up. In most cases, they will advise that you work up reasonably quickly to eating more calories than you would at a normal weight. This is often alarming to someone who has been living on a bare minimum for some time. There are very good reasons for this. You may also be advised to include fat in your diet, as fat is a significant provider of calories in a normal diet. This can be very hard, especially with such a societal obsession with low and no fat foods.

After a period of starvation, you will have lost valuable lean tissue (muscle) as well as body fat. When the body starts to lose lean tissue, it will slow down the metabolic rate (this is the speed at which the body burns food). It may be a surprise to know that for most people to gain just ½ kg (one pound) in weight, they will need to eat an extra 3,500 calories more than their normal food intake to keep their weight stable. This is the calorific equivalent of 10 Mars bars or 85 apples! (though you won't be asked to eat 10 Mars bars or 85 apples!!).

Researchers have found that individuals with anorexia need even more calories to put on any weight, because more food is required to kick-start the metabolic rate. Although more food is required in the earlier stages of recovery from anorexia, this is usually reduced as the person nears or reaches their normal range.

When you start to eat bigger amounts of food again, you may feel bloated and fatter. Although this can add to a feeling of being out of control of weight, it is very normal and to be expected. The bloated stomach can last for some time, but as you near your set-point range, the weight you have gained will be redistributed more evenly over your body.

When you start to put on weight again, you may feel hunger pangs stronger than ever, and fear that you will not be able to stop eating and will lose control and become fat. This is just the body's way of letting itself get back to a healthy weight and the hunger pangs should return to normal as you near a healthy weight range. It is in *no one's interests* to allow you to put on more weight than is within the set-point range, and careful monitoring is needed to ensure that weight is regained at a steady, gradual, reasonable rate.

As well as some of the physical effects of starting to eat again, you will have to learn to cope with other difficult emotions such as feeling out of control. You will probably have learnt to view food in a very negative way, as though it is something to be feared. You will probably have developed strict rules and beliefs about safe and unsafe foods to eat which will have made the range of foods you eat very limited. Starting to break free from these rules will feel very uncertain and scary, and a lot of support, encouragement and advice will be required to help you through this difficult phase.

Working towards a healthy set-point range can seem like the scariest part of recovering from anorexia. It is vital that you can share your concerns and have the support of a team of people, which will need to include family and carers, friends and professionals.

▶ Understanding anorexia

There are different types of therapies that may help you to understand more about anorexia and the effects it has on you and your family. In these therapies you will have the chance to express lots of different feelings and explore lots of different ideas.

▶ Family work

During these sessions, you will have the opportunity to discuss and explore issues with your family and therapist present. As part of this work, all family members will be invited to think about and contribute to discussions. Anorexia can often make clear communication within families very difficult, and through these sessions all family members will be supported to communicate with each other and think together about how to work against anorexia. Some of these sessions may focus on thinking about ways to solve problems or resolve conflicts as a family.

▶ Individual work

You may have the opportunity to do some individual work with a therapist. As part of this work you may learn new skills that will help you overcome your current problems and problems that you might face in the future. Individual work may also help you to understand more about your thoughts and how they can affect the way you feel and what you do.

▶ Group therapies/Self-help groups

Group therapy gives you a place where you can talk about your problems with other young people going through the same kind of difficulties. This may well help you to feel supported and understood by other young people in similar situations.

In these groups, you may have the chance to explore ideas about developing normal eating. Activities such as planning and cooking normal meals or choosing normal-sized clothes may form part of this. You could also talk about other things, for example, changing the way you live your life as well as what it is like growing up and becoming more independent.

My team

Who is already in your team and how can they help you?

Person   *Help they offer*

What other people might you need around you and what can they do?

Person   *What they can do*

How might anorexia get in the way of you working as a team and how could you overcome this?

Problem   *How to overcome this*

Becoming assertive

The way we communicate with others can have a huge impact on our relationships. Sometimes we chat with people whom we feel equal to and we talk in a confident and relaxed way. This kind of interaction helps us feel good about ourselves. Other times we may put ourselves down, feel as though we are not important and communicate in a very nervous and uncertain way. This may leave us feeling unheard and frustrated. Imagine your day being made up of lots of conversations of this second kind – you would be feeling pretty awful at the end of the day! Many people with eating disorders end up having lots of the second kind of interactions because they feel worthless.

In this section, we will be finding out what assertiveness is and learning some ways to help us become more assertive. Working on these skills will help to improve our relationships and our own self-esteem.

What is assertiveness?

What thoughts immediately jump into your head when you think about this question? Write them down below. We will come back to that question at the end to see if you feel any different.

Put very simply, assertiveness is:

1 Standing up for your RIGHTS in a way that you do not dis-respect other people's rights.

2 Expressing your needs, opinions, feelings, beliefs and wants in a DIRECT and HONEST way.

In any interaction we have with people, there are three main ways we can communicate:

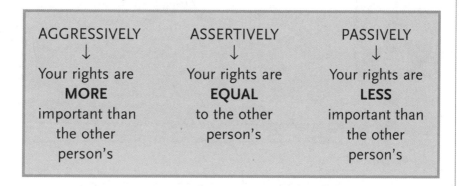

AGGRESSIVELY	ASSERTIVELY	PASSIVELY
↓	↓	↓
Your rights are **MORE** important than the other person's	Your rights are **EQUAL** to the other person's	Your rights are **LESS** important than the other person's

What would you do?

Say, for example, that you have just bought a CD that you've been really wanting. A friend asks if they can borrow it, but you haven't even taken it out of the bag!

> What would you do?
>
> ....
>
> ....
>
> ....
>
> ....

See if you can guess which of the different options below is an assertive, aggressive or passive response.

1 'OK, you take it, it doesn't matter that I've not listened to it yet.'

   ASSERTIVE   AGGRESSIVE   PASSIVE

2 'You must be joking! No way!'

   ASSERTIVE   AGGRESSIVE   PASSIVE

3 'Actually, I haven't listened to it myself yet. Can I give it to you in the next couple of days?'

   ASSERTIVE   AGGRESSIVE   PASSIVE

▶ Human rights

Everybody in the world has rights that they are entitled to.
Below is a charter of rights. Next to each statement is a box.
Tick the boxes if you believe this right applies to you and to
other people.

The right to be treated with respect as an equal human being

Other people   Myself

☐   ☐

The right to express my thoughts and feelings

Other people   Myself

☐   ☐

The right to say NO

Other people   Myself

☐   ☐

The right to make mistakes

Other people   Myself

☐   ☐

The right to choose not to take responsibility for other people

Other people   Myself

☐   ☐

*The right to be myself. This sometimes means being the same or
different from other people*

Other people   Myself

☐   ☐

Review your rights

Take a good look at the boxes you have ticked and think about the rights you feel you have or do not have. Notice where there are differences between yourself and others and how you might have developed this belief.

Pocket-size rights

My *rights*

Write on a small piece of card the rights above and add any others you can think of. Carry this around with you for a day, reminding yourself of these rights whenever you can. Imagine looking after these rights and keeping them safe by making sure that in all your interactions with other people, you protect them.

How did it feel to have these rights with you?

Did you manage to take care of them?

If not, what was difficult?

Try it again another day.

 Why be assertive?

Assertiveness is a skill that we need to learn and practise and, just like any other skill, it requires effort. So why bother?

▶ *You are more likely to get what you want out of life.*
When you are clear what your ideas and opinions are, it increases your chances of people being able to help you. Also, because assertiveness is about respecting other people's rights, it also gives them the opportunity to make their opinions known, so neither person is left feeling confused.

▶ *More confidence in yourself.*
Even when you don't get what you want, you can still feel OK about yourself if you were assertive. You are never left feeling, 'Why didn't I say that?' Going over what you 'should' have said makes you feel less confident about saying it another time. If you do manage to be assertive and are listened to, you get an enormous boost in confidence and will find it easier and easier to be assertive next time, and with other people. You may become less dependent on seeking the approval of others and trust your own opinions more.

▶ *Taking responsibility.*
Being assertive means taking more responsibility for your own behaviour. Therefore, you are likely to feel much more in control, than feeling pushed around by other people. When you have a greater sense of control over your life by being assertive, you may find it much easier to let go of using anorexia as a means of achieving a sense of control.

▶ *Save energy.*
Assertiveness breeds assertiveness; the more you do it, the easier it gets. This means less time taken up worrying about upsetting others, what you wish you'd said, or feeling angry at yourself or others.

Being assertive and being listened to can give you an enormous boost of confidence

▶ Why NOT be assertive?

So far it seems as though there are good reasons to be assertive and that it is quite easy to do. However, many people struggle to be assertive and protect their rights and express their feelings. There are often good reasons for this:

▶ *'Something bad will happen.'*
For example, you may worry that you will lose your friends if you say 'No' when they ask to copy your homework. Or you may worry about the conversation turning into an argument. These worries will go away. If you practise being assertive, you will find out that you can handle situations confidently. We can never predict how other people will respond, but it is *not* always our responsibility if they do get upset. Furthermore, we are more likely to upset other people by always trying to please other people – it's just impossible!

▶ *'I'm not entitled to the same rights as others.'*
You need to believe in your rights in order to stand up for them. We hold beliefs in our heads, e.g. 'I'll never be as good as them'. These influence the way we behave, for

example, not making eye contact with people, always apologising and letting others go first.

▶ *'Assertiveness really means being aggressive.'*
If we grow up with people who are either very passive or aggressive, we may be confused about what assertiveness is. Any direct statement may seem quite forceful and aggressive to a person who isn't used to people being assertive. Assertiveness isn't something we are born with, it has to be learned and practised. If we have grown up around people who have 'modelled' it for us, it is obviously much easier to learn. Otherwise it takes a lot of effort, but it is really worth it.

▶ *'It never worked in the past when I tried to let people know my feelings.'*
As already mentioned, being assertive does not always mean we get the reaction we want, but we give ourselves a much better chance of this by being clear and direct. If people are used to us being passive and going along with things, it sometimes takes time for them to step back and listen. We may have to keep repeating ourselves, and practise being assertive regularly, to make sure people respect our rights.

▶ *'Being passive is being polite.'*
We may have been brought up not to let our feelings show, to always agree with other people, and not to accept praise. These may all have been referred to as 'being polite'. It is possible to be polite and be assertive. If you're not sure how, watch your favourite TV programme and try to look out for characters that seem to get it right (and those who don't!).

▶ Developing assertiveness

There are three areas to focus on to become assertive: what you SAY, DO and THINK.

Assertive talk

▶ Use 'I' when you speak, so people are clear that it is your opinion: 'I would prefer it if we went to see the other film' rather than 'Let's see that film' or 'Maybe we could see the other film'.

▶ Don't apologise when you haven't done something wrong: 'I'm really sorry to say this, but could I have my CD back.'

▶ Don't put yourself down: 'I could go bowling, but I'm useless!'

Assertive behaviour

▶ Think about the tone of your voice. The way you say something is often just as important as what you have said.

▶ Speak loud enough for people to hear you.

▶ Make eye contact with the other person.

▶ Try not to put your hands over your mouth when speaking and hold your head straight on rather than looking down.

▶ Be aware of your body language: are you fidgeting?

Assertive thoughts

We have already mentioned how our beliefs about our rights can affect the way we behave. We often have a private conversation with ourselves that, if we listened to carefully, would tell us clearly how we view our rights. Take, for example, a class where the teacher has just told you to prepare a presentation. Immediately, you will start to have thoughts about it that rush through your mind and will make you feel and do different things. Look at how the different thoughts below affect feelings and actions:

Thought	Feeling	Action
I'm going to make such a fool of myself.	Panic	Biting nails Not sleeping
I can't believe she is asking us to do that.	Anger	Moan to friends Can't concentrate
I know I'll go red.	Embarrassment	Pretend to be ill Put hands in front of face
I'll give it a go. Everyone else is feeling nervous.	Nervous	Do lots of preparation
I get nervous but I've managed OK before when I've spoken in front of people.	Quite confident	Quite relaxed

If you can listen to the thoughts that go rushing through your mind, you can begin to challenge them. First you need to say a loud 'STOP' in your mind and put the thoughts on pause. Then you have time to think about it more clearly. It may be helpful to use some of the strategies in Section 8, 'Getting better', such as thinking about what a friend would say about the beliefs you hold about yourself.

▶ Some other useful tips

If you know in advance there is a situation where you may struggle to be assertive, take time to prepare yourself. Think about exactly what you want to say and what you feel your rights are. Then think about when would be a good time and where would be a good place to talk about the issue. Where and when can you make sure that you will be heard and not feel rushed? For example, trying to tell your mum something important in the middle of making tea is probably not the best idea, but suggesting you go out for a walk somewhere quiet may be easier.

How would you deal assertively with these situations?

1 You are in a rush to get out of the house when a friend knocks on the door. She wants your advice about something important to her.

2 You bought an expensive pair of trousers from a shop and after a week they have started falling apart!

3 A teacher criticises your work when you put a lot of effort into it.

4 You are having a conversation with someone who says something offensive about a friend.

5 Someone tells you they like your hair.

And finally . . . what is assertiveness?

Assertiveness is . . .

_____

_____

_____

_____

_____

Has your answer changed from the beginning of the chapter?

Myths and questions about anorexia nervosa

You may have heard many 'myths' or ideas about anorexia nervosa from newspapers, magazines and television. This section might help to clear up some common myths that people have about anorexia nervosa and answer some of the questions that you may have.

Only teenage girls suffer from eating disorders

Many eating disorders such as anorexia do begin in the teenage years. However, it can happen to younger children and older people too. It's not something that just young girls suffer from either, boys and men can also develop eating disorders.

You can never fully recover from anorexia

Overcoming anorexia isn't easy, but with hard work and determination from you, and the right kind of help and support from others, *it is possible*. Many people who have suffered with anorexia are now able to live completely normal lives.

Sometimes people are faced with new challenges after a period of time of being free from anorexia. They may return to anorexia as an old coping strategy. It is important to remember that these 'lapses' can be temporary and not to blame yourself. It's likely that the 'lapse' is due to a new trouble or situation you haven't faced before and you may need some more support to help you through.

Am I to blame for having anorexia?

You are NOT to blame for your eating disorder. There are many different reasons why someone develops anorexia. The 'trigger' for your eating disorder is likely to have made you feel out of control and anorexia 'sneaked' its way into your life as a way of managing.

However, you do have the choice now about what path you take. For example, you could hold on to your anorexia and keep it safe by allowing it to control your thoughts and behaviour. The other choice you have is to reject it and develop other ways of coping and take back control for yourself.

I don't think I really have anorexia. I'm not thin enough

People who suffer from anorexia will often find it difficult to accept that they have a problem because they don't feel thin enough or do not match some of the pictures they have seen of people with anorexia.

Sometimes this stops them from getting the right help because they fear they won't be thin enough or may even be sent away without any help or think that they don't deserve any help. Some people have anorexia and do not look extremely thin. Likewise, you may not have all the symptoms that have been mentioned in this book. The way that anorexia affects us varies from person to person.

How long does it take to get better from anorexia?

It is impossible to say how long it will take each person to make a full recovery from anorexia. Everyone is different and it is important that you work at your own pace. Unfortunately, it will not disappear overnight! It will take commitment and hard work, but with each difficult hurdle you overcome, you will be one step further away from anorexia and one step closer to getting your own life back.

Anorexics never eat

People with anorexia restrict the amount they eat, but will usually allow themselves to eat some 'safe' foods (usually foods that are low in calories and fat content). However, many people with anorexia occasionally binge on more high-energy foods like crisps and chocolate.

People cannot have more than one eating disorder

There are often many overlaps between eating disorders such as anorexia nervosa and bulimia nervosa. For example, someone with anorexia can also binge on food. It is important to remember that for all of the different eating disorders, the way food is used is just a symptom and not the actual problem.

Does vomiting or using laxatives after I've eaten mean I won't put on the calories?

Trying to rid your body of food that you have eaten either by being sick or using laxatives is NOT a successful strategy to stop your body from taking in calories. Most of the time you will not be able to rid yourself of all the food. Furthermore, your metabolism will become confused and may slow down. Vomiting or using laxatives could also have dangerous health effects and will leave you feeling tired. You will have also lost water that your body needs. This will leave you feeling very thirsty.

Every day I go on the scales my weight changes. Sometimes I put on weight after eating only a small amount of food. Why is this?

Weight is not something that remains stable, regardless of what you eat. There are many things that affect weight change, such as fluid retention, when your body holds on to fluid. Changes in hormones can also affect your weight and sometimes there are different levels of hormones in our bodies depending on the time of day, what you have eaten, or how much sleep you have had. It is very normal for weight to fluctuate around your set point, as mentioned earlier.

Sometimes when we have eaten only small amounts of food, our bodies will go into 'starvation mode' and take up more of the calories in the food than if we had eaten a larger meal. This is why sometimes people fail to lose weight even when they are eating small amounts of food.

Many people with eating disorders weigh themselves a number of times each day. They believe that small increases or decreases mean that they have put on or lost weight. This can affect their whole day, even though it is extremely unlikely that the number on the scales was a true reflection of their actual weight.

> **If I get help for my anorexia, I just know they'll make me fat and I'll feel out of control**

Starting to get help for anorexia can be an extremely frightening time. You will be working on changing many of the anorexic habits, such as starting to eat normal meals again. Professionals are there to help and support you and talk about the fears you have. Their aim is to get you healthy again, NOT fat. Anorexia can make it difficult for you to trust these people, but it is essential that you work with them to beat anorexia.

> **People with anorexia are attention-seekers**

People usually develop eating disorders because they have experienced some difficult times in their lives and they have found it hard to cope with these experiences. Food and eating become a substitute for the lack of control they feel they have. Most people with anorexia would say that it is an extremely unpleasant disorder to experience and would want to change it if they knew how.

No one with anorexia simply starves him- or herself to gain attention. However, sufferers sometimes receive positive comments about their weight loss in the very early stages, which can give them a sense of achievement and add to a feeling of being in control.

> **People choose to be anorexic, so they could give it up if they wanted**

Anorexia is very clever in who it targets. It tends to choose young people who have high expectations of themselves, but do not necessarily feel as though they meet their expectations. It is extremely rare that anyone chooses to be anorexic; rather, anorexia gradually takes over control of them. Also, once anorexia has got a grip of the way that the person thinks and behaves, it is very hard to battle against it alone. It takes a lot of hard work and support from people who understand.

Your own questions

As you're now nearing the end of this workbook, think about any questions you have. Write them down and think about how you might answer them. For example, you might have a person you could talk to, a book, or the Net. If you do use the Net, it might be worthwhile checking out the information with a parent/carer or a professional. Just because it's on the Net doesn't mean it's right. Anyone can put things on the Net and it can sound very clever – but be careful because it could be wrong.

Some good advice and messages of support

'I managed to separate my feelings from food!'

Emily, 17 years old

'No matter what the voices threw at me, I countered it with a healthy message. I'm not saying it was easy. To begin with I remembered what the therapist had told me, my healthy voice was a mere whisper. Gradually it became stronger and had conviction when it spoke.'

Heather, 19 years old

'I realised I had two choices:

1 I could hold onto the eating disorder, stop fighting and give into it.

OR

2 I could make the decision to let go of the eating disorder, fight it daily, and receive help and treatment.

I opted for the second choice, knowing that for a period of time I would continue to feel bad, if not worse, but eventually things would seem brighter.'

Sara, 17 years old

'Relapses are part of recovery. Have the courage to be imperfect!'

Josh, 17 years old

'The more I allowed anorexia to be heard, the stronger it became. I would scream at it at times to stop it pounding my brain.'

Clare, 12 years old

'My diary became a tool so that I could honestly express my feelings and make sense of some of the thoughts that I thought were too irrational to voice.'

Harry, 15 years old

'You have the right to any feelings you have. You have the right to express them to the person hurting you, making you angry or frustrated or even making you happy!'

Lindsey, 16 years old

'I ate at set times whether I was hungry or not and rewarded myself with things I enjoy doing.'

Kate, 13 years old

157

'I chose to devote more time to recovery from anorexia than maintaining starvation.'

James, 16 years old

'Keeping a journal was a big part of my recovery. When I found myself not wanting to eat or thinking I was a "fat pig", I would stop and look at my feelings to find out what was really making me feel so bad.'

Lucy, 14 years old

'I'm no longer anorexic, I'm human!! It is human to doubt yourself, be unsure, have a bad hair day! Everyone has weight fluctuations. The point is not to link these changes with my self-worth. I choose to concentrate on the changes within myself. Every day I grow and learn new things about myself and the world around me.'

Nita, 16 years old

'I practised communicating in the mirror!'

Eve, 17 years old

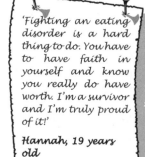
'Fighting an eating disorder is a hard thing to do. You have to have faith in yourself and know you really do have worth. I'm a survivor and I'm truly proud of it!'

Hannah, 19 years old

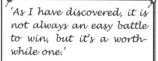
'Just DO IT. There will never be a "right time".'

Mohammed, 13 years old

'I wrote down on index cards the healthy ways to deal with difficult situations. I also wrote reminders about myself, like "I am a good person", and I kept them handy.'

Marie, 14 years old

'As I have discovered, it is not always an easy battle to win, but it's a worthwhile one.'

Rebecca, 13 years old

'I put away my scales and measuring tape and gave away my "skinny" clothes.'

Annie, 15 years old

'In treatment I began to notice small changes in my thinking and I sensed that somewhere I had the ability to think differently about myself.'

Kirsty, 14 years old

'I was really frightened I wouldn't be able to stop eating and felt I was failing at being an anorexic. But that changes and I can stop eating and there are no awards for being the best anorexic out there!'

Tara, 13 years old

'I'm no longer preoccupied by food or fearful of it. I can experience life! I've missed so much but I'm excited about my future.'

Dan, 18 years old

'It is possible to beat your eating disorder but you have to understand the illness and why it developed.'

Harriet, 14 years old

'All the people of the world are different and we're supposed to be that way.'

Henry, 17 years old

'Life is too short! Make every day count, and always remember tomorrow is worth fighting for.'

Teresa, 16 years old

The final task!

▶ Write your own message of inspiration

Congratulations! You've reached the end of the *Hunger for Understanding* workbook. Therefore, you've already taken a huge step towards getting better. You hopefully know more about the true facts of anorexia and understand the games it can play. What do you think are the most important messages you will be taking with you from the book? You may want to write a message to yourself that will help you in difficult times. Keep this somewhere close and safe so that it is there when you need it.

Good luck!!!!

Useful contacts

After reading this manual you may want to find out more about eating disorders in young people and mental health issues in general. Listed below are the names and addresses of some websites that will help you do this.

▶ Eating disorders

ANAD

National Association of Anorexia Nervosa and Associated Disorders provides information and resources about anorexia nervosa and other associated disorders.

Website: www.anad.org

ANRED

Anorexia Nervosa and Related Eating Disorders provides information and resources on anorexia nervosa, bulimia nervosa and other less-well-known eating disorders.

Website: www.anred.com

EDA

The Eating Disorders Association offers help, support and advice on eating disorders.

Address: 103 Prince of Wales Road
             Norwich
             NR1 1DW
Telephone: 0845 634 1414 (Helpline open 8.30 am to 8.30 pm weekdays
             and 1.00 pm to 4.30 pm Saturday)
             0845 634 7650 (Callers 18 and under: open 4.00 pm to 6.30 pm
             weekdays and 1.00 pm to 4.30 pm Saturday)
Website: www.edauk.com

▶ General mental health for young people

Mental Health Foundation
The Mental Health Foundation works with children and young people with common mental health difficulties.

Address: UK Office
             7th Floor
             83 Victoria Street
             London
             SW1H 0HW
Telephone: 0207 802 0300
Website: www.mentalhealth.org.uk

NAMI
The Nation's Voice on Mental Illness provides comprehensive information on what is anorexia nervosa.

Website: www.nami.org

Young Minds
This organisation aims to improve the mental health of all children and young people.

Address: 102–108 Clerkenwell Road
             London
             EC1M 5SA
Telephone: 0207 336 8445
Website: www.youngminds.org.uk

▶ The disturbing trend of pro-anorexia websites

Pro-anorexia websites are websites that promote eating disorders. They provide information that helps young people engage in unhealthy practices that can contribute to mental health difficulties. As more and more people are becoming aware of these sites, service providers are being pressured into removing them – so they are becoming fewer!

If you have concerns about pro-anorexia websites, you can contact SCARED – Support Concern and Resources for Eating Disorders at www.eating-disorder.org.

References

American Psychiatric Association (1999a) Treatment principles and alternatives. Retrieved 30 January 2001, from http://www.psych.org/clin_res/guide.bk-5cfm.

American Psychiatric Association (1999b) Developing a treatment plan for the individual patient. Retrieved 30 January 2001, from http://www.psych.org/clin_res/guide.bk-5cfm.

Bell, L. (2002) Does concurrent psychopathology at presentation influence response to treatment for bulimia nervosa? *Eating and Weight Disorders*, **7**, 168–181.

Bell, L., Clare, L. and Thorn, E. (2000) *Service Guidelines for People with Eating Disorders*. The British Psychological Society, Division of Clinical Psychology, occasional paper No. 3. London: BPS.

Beutler, L.E., Machado, P.P.P. and Neufeldt, S.A. (1994) Therapist variables. In A.E. Bergin and S.L. Garfield (eds) *Handbook of Psychotherapy and Behaviour Change* (4th edn), pp. 229–269. New York: John Wiley & Sons.

Blake, W., Turnball, S. and Treasure, J. (1997) Stages and process of change in eating disorders: implication for therapy. *Clinical Psychology and Psychotherapy*, **4**, 186–191.

Bruch, H. (1962) Perceptual and conceptual disturbances in anorexia nervosa. *Psychosomatic Medicine*, **24**, 187–194.

Bruch, H. (1973) *Eating Disorders: Obesity, Anorexia Nervosa and the Person Within*. New York: Basic Books.

Carr, A. (1999) *The Handbook of Child and Adolescent Clinical Psychology: A Contextual Approach*. London: Routledge.

Channon, S., de Silva, P., Hemsley, D. and Perkins, R. (1989) A controlled trial of cognitive behavioural and behavioural treatment of anorexia nervosa. *Behavioural Research and Therapy*, **27**, 529–535.

Crisp, A.H. (1997) Anorexia nervosa as a flight from growth: assessment and treatment based on the model. In D.M. Garner and P.E. Garfinkel (eds) *Handbook for Treatment of Eating Disorders* (2nd edn). New York: Guilford Press.

Crisp, A.H., Norton, K.W.R., Gowers, S.G., Halek, C., Levett, G., Yeldham, D., Bowyer, C. and Bhat, A. (1991) A controlled study of the effect of therapies aimed at adolescent and family psychopathology in Anorexia Nervosa. *British Journal of Psychiatry*, **159**, 325–333.

Dare, C., Eilser, I., Russell, G., Treasure, J. and Dodge, L. (2001) Psychological therapies for adults with anorexia nervosa: randomised controlled trial of outpatient treatments. *British Journal of Psychiatry*, **178**, 216–221.

Eating Disorders Association (1994) *Eating Disorders: A Guide to Purchasing and Providing Services*. Norwich: EDA.

Ebeling, H., Tapanainen, P., Joutsenoja, A., Koskinen, M., Morin-Papunen, L., Jarvi, L., Hassinen, R., Keski-Rahkonen, A., Rissanen, A. and Wahlbeck, K. (2003) *Prac-

tice Guidelines for the Treatment of Eating Disorders in Children and Adolescents. Helsinki: Finnish Medical Association.

Eilser, I., Dare, C., Russell, G.F.M., Szmukler, G., Le Grange, D. and Dodge, E. (1997) Family and individual therapy in Anorexia Nervosa, a five-year follow up. *Archives of General Psychiatry*, **54**, 1025–1030.

Eivors, A., Button, E., Warner, S. and Turner, K. (2003) Understanding the experience of dropout from treatment for anorexia nervosa. *European Eating Disorders Review*, **11**, 90–107.

Engel, K. and Wilms, H. (1986) Therapy motivation in anorexia nervosa: theory and first empirical results. *Psychotherapy and Psychosomatics*, **46**, 161–170.

Freeman, C. (2002) *Overcoming Anorexia Nervosa: A Self-help Guide Using Cognitive-behavioural Techniques.* London: Constable and Robinson.

Garner, D.M., Garfinkel, P.E. and Bemis, K.M. (1982) A multidimensional psychotherapy for anorexia nervosa. *International Journal of Eating Disorders*, **1**, 3–46.

Garner, D.M., Vitousek, K.M. and Pike, K.M. (1997) Cognitive-behavioural therapy for anorexia nervosa. In D.M. Garner and P.E. Garfinkel (eds) *Handbook of Treatment for Eating Disorders.* New York: Guilford Press.

Gowers, S. and Bryant-Waugh, R. (2004) Management of child and adolescent eating disorders: the current evidence base and future directions. *Journal of Child Psychology and Psychiatry*, **45**(1), 63–83.

Herzog, D.B., Norman, D.K., Gordon, C. and Penpose, M. (1984) Sexual conflict and eating disorders in 27 males. *American Journal of Psychiatry*, **141**, 989–994.

Hsu, G.L.K., Crisp, A.H. and Callender, J.S. (1992) Recovery in anorexia nervosa: the patient's perspective. *International Journal of Eating Disorders*, **11**(4), 341–350.

Jacobs, B. and Isaacs, S. (1986) Pre-puberty anorexia nervosa: a retrospective controlled study. *Journal of Child Psychology and Psychiatry*, **27**, 237–250.

Kazdin, A.E. and Weisz, J.R. (1998) Identifying and developing empirically supported child and adolescent treatments. *Journal of Consulting and Clinical Psychology*, **66**, 19–36.

Keesey, R.E. (1993) Physiological regulation of body energy: implications for obesity. In A.J. Stunkard and T.A. Wadden (eds) *Obesity: Theory and Therapy* (2nd edn), pp. 77–96. New York: Raven Press.

Keys, A., Brozek, J., Henschel, A., Mickelson, O. and Taylor, H.L. (1950) *The Biology of Human Starvation.* Minneapolis: University of Minnesota.

Klerman, G.L., Weissman, M.M., Rounsaville, B.J. and Chervon, E.S. (1984) *Interpersonal Psychotherapy of Depression.* New York: Basic Books.

Kreipe, R.E., Golden, N.H., Katzman, D.K., et al. (1995) Eating disorders in adolescents: a position paper of the Society for Adolescent Medicine. *Journal of Adolescent Health*, **16**, 476–479.

Le Grange, D., Eisler, I., Dare, C. and Russell, G.F.M. (1992) Evaluation of family therapy in anorexia nervosa: a pilot study. *International Journal of Eating Disorders*, **12**, 347–357.

Le Grange, D. and Gelman, T. (1998) Patient's perspective of treatment in eating disorders: a preliminary study. *South African Journal of Psychology*, **28**(3), 182–186.

Luborsky, L., McLellan, A.T., Woody, G.E., O'Brien, C.P. and Auberbach, A. (1985) Therapist success and its determinants. *Archives of General Psychiatry*, **42**, 602–611.

Miller, W.R. (1983) Motivational interviewing with problem drinkers. *Behavioural Psychotherapy*, **11**, 147–172.

Miller, W.R. and Rollnick, S. (1991) *Motivational Interviewing: Preparing People to Change Addictive Behaviour*. New York: Guilford Press.

Miller, W.R. and Rollnick, S. (2002) *Motivational Interviewing: Preparing People to Change Addictive Behaviour* (2nd edn). New York: Guilford Press.

Minuchin, S., Rosman, B.L. and Baker, L. (1978) *Psychosomatic Families: Anorexia Nervosa in Context*. Cambridge, MA: Harvard University Press.

Neilson, S., Moller-Madsen, S., Isager, T., et al. (1998) Standardised mortality in eating disorders: quantitative summary of previously published and new evidence. *Journal of Psychosomatic Research*, **44**, 412–434.

NICE (2004) *Eating Disorders: Core Interventions in the Treatment and Management of Anorexia Nervosa, Bulimia Nervosa and Related Eating Disorders: A National Clinical Practice Guideline*. London: National Institute of Clinical Excellence.

Norris, D.L. (1984) The effects of mirror confrontation on self-estimation of body dimensions in anorexia nervosa, bulimia and two control groups. *Psychological Medicine*, **14**, 835–842.

Palazzoli, M.S. (1978) *Self-starvation: From the Intrapsychic to the Intrapersonal Approach to Anorexia Nervosa*. New York: Aronson.

Palmer, R.L. and Treasure, J. (1999) Providing specialised services for anorexia nervosa. *British Journal of Psychiatry*, **175**, 306–309.

Prochaska, J.O. and DiClemente, C.C. (1992) The transtheoretical approach. In J.C. Norcross and I.L. Goldfield (eds) *Handbook of Psychotherapy Integration*, pp. 300–334. New York: Basic Books.

Prochaska, J.O., Norcross, J.C. and DiClemente, C.C. (1994) *Changing for Good*. New York: William Morrow.

Roth, A. and Fonagy, P. (1996) *What Works for Whom: A Critical Review of Psychotherapy Research*. New York: Guilford Press.

Royal College of Psychiatrists (2000) *Eating Disorders in the UK: Policies for Service Development and Training*. Council Report CR87. London: Royal College of Psychiatrists.

Russell, G.F., Szmukler, G.I., Darce, C., et al. (1987) An evaluation of family therapy in anorexia nervosa and bulimia nervosa. *Archives of General Psychiatry*, **44**, 1047–1056.

Stallard, P. (2002) *Think Good – Feel Good: A Cognitive Behaviour Therapy Workbook for Children and Young People*. Chichester: John Wiley & Sons.

Szmukler, D. and Dare, C. (1991) The Maudsley Hospital study of family therapy in anorexia nervosa and bulimia nervosa. In B. Woodside and L. Shelkter-Wolfson (eds) *Family Approaches in Treatment of Eating Disorders*. Washington, DC: APA.

Szmukler, G. and Patton, G. (1995) Sociocultural models of eating disorders. In G. Szmukler, C. Dare and J. Treasure (eds) *Handbook of Eating Disorders*. Chichester: John Wiley & Sons.

Treasure, J.L., Katzman, M., Schmidt, U., Troop, N., Todd, G. and deSilva, P. (1999) Engagement and outcome in the treatment of bulimia nervosa: first phase of a sequential design comparing motivation enhancement therapy and cognitive behavioural therapy. *Behaviour Research and Therapy*, **37**, 405–418.

Treasure, J., Todd, G., Brolly, M., et al. (1995) A pilot study of a randomised trial of cognitive analytic therapy vs. educational behaviour therapy for adult anorexia nervosa. *Behaviour Research and Therapy*, **33**, 363–367.

Wallace, S.A., Crown, J.M., Cox, A.D. and Berger, M. (1995) *Epidemiologically-based Needs Assessment: Child and Adolescent Mental Health.* Winchester: Wessex Institute of Public Health.

Ward, A., Troop, N., Todd, G. and Treasure, J. (1996) To change or not to change – 'How?' is the question. *British Journal of Medical Psychology,* **69**, 139–146.

Williams, G.J., Power, K.G., Millar, H.R., Freeman, C.P., Yellowless, S., Dowds, T., Walker, M., Campsie, L., MacPherson, F. and Jackson, M.A. (1993) Comparison of eating disorders and other dietary/weight groups on measures of perceived control, assertiveness, self-esteem and self-directed hostility. *International Journal of Eating Disorders,* **14**(1), 27–32.

Wilson, G.T. and Fairburn, C.G. (1998) Treatment for eating disorders. In P.E. Nathan and J.M. Gorman (eds) *Guide to Treatments that Work.* New York: Oxford University Press.

Index